McTEAGUE: A Tale of San Francisco

Neal Bell
adapted from the novel by
Frank Norris

BROADWAY PLAY PUBLISHING INC
New York
www.broadwayplaypublishing.com
info@broadwayplaypublishing.com

McTEAGUE

© Copyright 1992 by Neal Bell

First published by B P P I in *Plays by Neal Bell* in August 1998
This edition, first printing: March 2017
I S B N: 978-0-88145-706-3

Book design: Marie Donovan
Page make-up: Adobe InDesign
Typeface: Palatino

McTEAGUE was commissioned by, and received
its world premiere at Berkeley Repertory Theater
(Sharon Ott, Artistic Director; Susan Medak, Managing
Director), opening in January 1992 with the following
cast and creative contributors:

MCTEAGUE	Jeffrey King
TRINA	Melissa Fraser Brown
MARCUS	Charles Dean
MISS BAKER	Barbara Oliver
GRANNIS	Mark Isaac Epstein
MARIA	Mia Katigbak
ZERKOW	Steven Anthony Jones
MOTHER	Ronnie Gilbert
FANCY DENTIST/LOTTERY AGENT/ POSTMAN/CRIBBENS	L Peter Callender

Director	Sharon Ott
Sets	George Tsypin
Costumes	Lydia Tanji
Lighting	James F Ingalls
Original music	Bruce Odland
Sound design	Stephen LeGrand
Scenic projection design	Charles Rose
Production stage manager	Meryl Lind Shaw
Production assistant	Terry Dawn McGlynn
Assistant director	Richard Corley
Fight consultant	Morgan Strickland
Production dramaturg	James Leverett

The author would like to thank Mame Hunt, who
helped to initiate this project.

McTEAGUE was subsequently presented—in its current, revised version—by the Duke University Drama Program, opening on 18 February 1994,with the following cast and creative contributors:

MCTEAGUE... Ari Fliakos
TRINA.. Victoria Vézquez
MARCUS..David Horowitz
MISS BAKER...Jamie C Simpson
GRANNIS.. Tommy Story
MARIA.. Karla Doble
ZERKOW.. Johnny Gou
MOTHER...Emily Culver
FANCY DENTIST/LOTTERY AGENT/
POSTMAN/CRIBBENS ....David Kneip

Director..Jody McAuliffe
Sets... Wenhai Ma
Costumes... Maria Savitsky
Lighting.. Tina Gallegos
Sound ....Tuck Satterfield
Fight choreography ....Stephen Schilling
Stage manager..Jennifer Marik

CHARACTERS & SETTING

McTEAGUE, *a big, young dentist*
TRINA, McTEAGUE's *wife*
MARCUS, *best friend of* McTEAGUE's
MISS BAKER, *an elderly woman who lives in* McTEAGUE's
building
GRANNIS, *an elderly veterinarian, who lives next door to*
  MISS BAKER
MARIA, *a Mexican woman who works as maid in*
  McTEAGUE's *building*
ZERKOW, *a junk-shop dealer, formerly a miner*
MOTHER, TRINA's *mother*
FANCY DENTIST/LOTTERY AGENT/POSTMAN/CRIBBENS,
an old miner (*)

San Francisco

The 1890s

(*) *These four parts were intended to be played by the same
actor, so* McTEAGUE *can be performed by a company of
five men and four women*

ACT ONE

(1)

(The one-room dental parlor of DR MCTEAGUE*)*

*(*MCTEAGUE—*a big, young man—has just finished his Sunday dinner and downed a pitcher of beer. Content, he rests in his dental chair, a concertina forgotten in his lap.)*

(In a cage nearby, a canary begins to sing.)

MCTEAGUE: Hey, bird.

(The bird sings.)

MCTEAGUE: Birdie, birdie, birdie…

(The bird trills on.)

MCTEAGUE: Singing, huh?

(More bird song)

*(*MCTEAGUE *picks up the concertina, starts to play and sing, extremely loudly:)*

MCTEAGUE:
Did you ever hear tell of sweet Betsy from Pike,
Who crossed the wide prairies with her lover Ike—

(From elsewhere in the apartment building, tenants yell:)

TENANT 1: *(Off)* McTeague!

TENANT 2: *(Off)* Yer rattlin' the winda-panes!

(Pause. MCTEAGUE *sings, softer but still quite loud:)*

McTEAGUE:
"—with two yoke of cattle and one spotted hog,
A tall Shanghai rooster and an old yeller dog."

TENANT 3: *(Off)* You woke the baby!

TENANT 4: *(Off)* Bite it off!

(Pause. Much softer, MCTEAGUE sings on:)

McTEAGUE: "The alkali desert was burning and bare,
And Isaac's soul shrank from the death that lurked
   there:
`Dear old Pike County, I'll go back to you.'
Says Betsy, `You'll go by yourself if you do'."

(By now MCTEAGUE is drifting off. The concertina slips from his hand, with a final bleat when it hits the floor. He belches.)

(A look of great contentment crosses MCTEAGUE's face, as he falls asleep. The canary warbles on.)

(2)

(The dental parlor)

(MCTEAGUE is using his fingers to pull the tooth of his patient MARCUS, a rough, young dandy who's pinned to the dental chair.)

(Behind them MISS BAKER, an elderly lady, is nervously waiting her turn.)

McTEAGUE: Hold on, if it hurts. Hold ON.

(MARCUS suddenly grabs the dentist's shoulder. MISS BAKER flinches.)

MISS BAKER: Doctor McTeague...

McTEAGUE: *(Not looking up)* Huh?

MISS BAKER: I could come back later, perhaps. When you aren't so taxed—

MCTEAGUE: This mug is the last I got. And then you. Sit tight. *(He turns to his work.)* Almost home, al...most...there. *(He steps back from his patient, holding up the bloody tooth he's pulled.)*

(Appalled, MISS BAKER *slips out of the room, unnoticed.)*

MARCUS: *(Stunned)* You pulled it?

*(*MCTEAGUE *nods.)*

MARCUS: I thought you was gettin' it ready or somethin'. You pulled it with your *fingers*?

MCTEAGUE: My father worked in a mine. I worked alongside. Trundlin' ore. Developed the hands.

MARCUS: Surprised you don't use a pick-axe, then.

MCTEAGUE: Did I hurt you? Huh?

MARCUS: I been to fancier dental parlors, tell ya the truth, and shelled out twice as much, and been stung a lot worse.

MCTEAGUE: The swanky doctors give you gas?

*(*MARCUS *nods.)*

MCTEAGUE: Did you check for your wallet after? *(Pause)* That's whatchacall "dental humor."

(Pause. MARCUS *laughs.)*

MARCUS: Doctor McTeague, yer all right. Let me buy you a beer.

MCTEAGUE: Afraid I got one more molar.

MARCUS: *(Looking around)* Not now you don't.

*(*MCTEAGUE *looks around and sees that* MISS BAKER *has flown.)*

MCTEAGUE: You know anybody who likes a dentist?

MARCUS: I might. *(He looks at his tooth, amazed.)* You popped this fang with your mitts? That's outa sight.

McTEAGUE: We're neighbors, ain't we? Don't you live on the floor above?

MARCUS: Since circumstances reduced me, yes. Come on. Take me up on the suds.

(Pause)

McTEAGUE: Long as yer buying.

(3)

(Frenna's Saloon)

(MARCUS and McTEAGUE down their beers as they stand at the door of the bar.)

MARCUS: Lookin' out for a friend?

McTEAGUE: I like to watch the people pass.

MARCUS: Ever wonder where they're going?

McTEAGUE: I don't.

MARCUS: I guess they know. *(Pause)* Back to empty rooms, how many, you ever wonder?

(McTEAGUE shakes his head.)

MARCUS: Sit alone in the dark. Gnash their teeth. Sometimes I figure it's tens of thousands. And then there's times I reckon it's only me. *(Pause. He looks at McTEAGUE.)* Penny?

McTEAGUE: Somethin' for nothing. I got no thoughts.

MARCUS: —which is just the way they want it.

McTEAGUE: Who?

(MARCUS points out at the street.)

MARCUS: The owners. Plutocrats in their shining beavers. Riding over the mud like us. *(He shouts:)* Try walkin' sometime, ya lard-cans, jeez!

McTEAGUE: Don't anybody own me.

MARCUS: —they would like you to think. Long as you stay in your place and keep quiet. Present your butt to be kicked when they need it. Lick the boot when the boot descends.

MCTEAGUE: I useta be worser off than I am.

MARCUS: Who wasn't? They let us crawl to a certain altitude. Gives `em the pleasure of cutting us off at the knees, when we try to stand.

MCTEAGUE: You an agitator?

MARCUS: I'm agitated. It's how I am, that's all. It ain't a profession. Professionally, I walk sick dogs for a vet on Polk Street.

MCTEAGUE: Grannis?

MARCUS: The very same. He a patient?

(MCTEAGUE *nods.*)

MARCUS: My old man was a vet. I learned some things. Not a lot. *(Pause)* I never could get the hang of college. You?

(Pause)

MCTEAGUE: I never got near enough to hang. This traveling dental fellow wandered up to our mining camp. Had as much schooling, I guess, as his donkey. Used a pair of rusty pliers. Yanked an entire bucket of teeth. Got a bucket of gold dust back. And the night this jawsmith packed his tent, my mother said I was going with him. My father'd already died of drink. She grabbed me, every word she shook me: "This is your very last chance." *(Pause)* "This is your very last chance."

(Pause)

MARCUS: So now yer your own man, now.

MCTEAGUE: I am.

MARCUS: You got your own dental "parlors"—

McTEAGUE: I do.

MARCUS: —cramped as your "parlors" is, one room, where you eat and sleep and work and fart, and forget to change the bedding, don'tcha, and lie in your chair of a Sunday, stupefied, ain't it, gizzard full and warm and dumb and what more do you want?

McTEAGUE: Not a thing.

MARCUS: Never let it be said, you don't dream big.

McTEAGUE: I don't dream in any wise.

MARCUS: —which is *also* the way they like it.

BARTENDER: *(Off)* Last call!

(MARCUS starts to exit.)

McTEAGUE: You up in the early hours?

MARCUS: Not being a railroad magnet yet. Walk a buncha rheumatical three-legged deaf-and-dumb balding dogs with terrible breath. Which ain't my dream.

McTEAGUE: What is? —if you got us all pegged.

(Pause)

MARCUS: To hell with you. *(He walks away.)*

McTEAGUE: *(Insistent)* What is?

(MARCUS stops.)

MARCUS: You wanta tramp out to the water tomorrow? I walk the dogs as far as the Cliff House steps. And then I ride the trolley home. And the dogs get to run alongside, it's a laugh, they get so lathered up and frantic—

McTEAGUE: Ain't tomorrow Sunday? Sunday I rest.

MARCUS: Choke on yer beer, McTeague.

(MARCUS *wanders off, as* MCTEAGUE—*alone now—finishes off his glass.*)

MCTEAGUE: Don't agitate *me*, you soap-box spouter. Don't I get to rest?

(4)

(*The dental parlor.* MCTEAGUE *is nodding off in his chair.*)

(MARIA, *a Mexican woman, knocks and enters, feather-duster in hand.*)

MARIA: You got any junk?

MCTEAGUE: You asked last week.

MARIA: Last week? Listen: Turn your back, things wear out in a *day*. (*She picks something up from the dentist's instrument tray.*) You got no need for this measly scrap of tin.

MCTEAGUE: That tape is gold. For fillings. I got no junk.

MARIA: None?

(MCTEAGUE *shakes his head. Reluctantly,* MARIA *puts down the tape.*)

MARIA: Then I dust. (*She gets to work.*)

MCTEAGUE: It's Sunday. Come back later.

MARIA: No, Sunday is fine. God don't care when I work. I got to eat. (*She dusts.*) You eat?

MCTEAGUE: Just now, at the coffee-joint. A chop. And suet-pudding, as long as yer askin'. And then I had me a pipe. And then I had *quiet*. Go AWAY.

MARIA: It's very quiet. Listen: no Nob Hill ladies shoppin' and chitterin' cross the street, the children ain't off to school and poundin' each other, dogs are letting each other lay, no wagons clatter by... Close your eyes. Let me finish my work. Only sound my duster makes is wind... (*As she talks, she moves closer and closer to the piece of gold dental tape.*)

McTEAGUE: (*Eyes closed*) Hear that honk?

MARIA: That's geese at the market. Two blocks over. That's how quiet you want, and it is. Drift away...

(McTEAGUE *seems to be dozing off.* MARIA *reaches out for the tape, but he—eyes closed—starts talking again. Fuming, she jerks back her hand.*)

McTEAGUE: Way far off...I hear a train...

MARIA: You ever sleep on a train?

McTEAGUE: Once. I was just a kid...

MARIA: They say you never sleep better. Do you? Rock a little, rock a little, clickety-clack and clickety-clack, always headin' west...

McTEAGUE: That's right.

MARIA: Always headin' west.

McTEAGUE: Till you hit the water.

MARIA: What if there was a bridge across? Keep on goin'. Over the water. Racin' the sun. Across the water. Always headin' west...always headin' west...

(McTEAGUE *is almost out.* MARIA's *about to pocket the dental gold, when we hear the racket of dozens of barking dogs outside.*)

(MARCUS *bursts into the room, and* MARIA *retreats in alarm.*)

MARCUS: McTeague!

McTEAGUE: (*Woozy*) Who wants `im?

MARCUS: Get outa that torture-device, you lazy duck! We're walking the dogs.

(5)

(At Cliff House, overlooking the ocean.)

*(*MARCUS *and* MCTEAGUE, *out of breath, rush on.)*

MARCUS: *(Calling an offstage dog)* Sheba! Heel!

MCTEAGUE: Aw, let her run. Stumble. Whatever a one-eyed mutt in a hurry'd do.

MARCUS: You don't think the dogs I walk'll follow orders? Sheba—raise you leg and let fly on the Cliff House porch! *(He watches.)* Good dog!

MCTEAGUE: *(Looking out)* All that yappin'. We musta picked up a few strays.

MARCUS: That ain't entirely doggy barks. See down below on the rocks?

MCTEAGUE: It's foggy.

MARCUS: Wait for a break.

MCTEAGUE: *(Peering)* Somethin flippin' and glistenin'—seals! Sheba, come look.

MARCUS: Don't call a one-eyed dog to the edge of a cliff.

*(*MCTEAGUE *looks out.)*

MCTEAGUE: That rock far out?

MARCUS: The jagged one the light is catching?

MCTEAGUE: Looks like a giant incisor.

MARCUS: Does it? *(They study the rock.)* You oughta get hold of a tooth that big. Hang it outside your parlor window. Shine like that.

MCTEAGUE: *(Entranced)* Paint it gold.

MARCUS: *Make* it gold. Gold paint never lasts.

MCTEAGUE: What does?

MARCUS: I woulda said love, till late last week. When my fiancee run off with a car-conductor.

McTEAGUE: Which line?

(MARCUS *gives* McTEAGUE *a look.*)

MARCUS: It don't matter which *line*. I already got another girl.

McTEAGUE: Engagin' this one too?

MARCUS: Not rich enough.

McTEAGUE: Huh.

MARCUS: But somethin' to look at. Long black hair, like a queen of somethin'. Skin like milk. She's a cousin. (*He looks off to the side:*) Sheba! Bad dog! Back offa that baby! (*To the babys offstage mother:*) Sorry! (*To* McTEAGUE:) You got a girl?

McTEAGUE: I work. And then it's Sunday. (*Pause*) You never know what women're thinking.

MARCUS: You don't even know *if* theyre thinkin'. (*Pause*) My cousin's got a friend. Dolores. Not so bad, when the light is dim. You wanta come out for a picnic Sunday?

McTEAGUE: My father said women was like a clam turned inside out. Soft on the outside, hard as rocks deep down.

MARCUS: Your father died of drink, remember.

McTEAGUE: Sundays I rest.

MARCUS: Not always, bunky. Look at today. It's Sunday and here you are.

McTEAGUE: A fluke.

MARCUS: Things change. They go on changing. (*He looks off:*) Sheba! Put that baby down! (*He runs off.*)

McTEAGUE: I ain't goin on any picnic!

(MCTEAGUE *looks out at the water.*)

(*He starts to imitate the seals, barking and clapping his hands.*)

(6)

(*The dental parlor*)

(MCTEAGUE *is asleep in his chair.*)

(*Above him, a giant golden tooth appears.*)

(*He smiles in his sleep, shifting position.*)

(*Suddenly, someone starts to bang on the door.*)

MARCUS: (*Off*) You in there, Mac?

(*The golden tooth disappears.*)

(MCTEAGUE *sits up, confused.*)

MARCUS: (*Off*) Mac? My cousin fell on the trolley-step! She's holdin' her tooth in her hand!

MCTEAGUE: It's open! Tell her to wait in the hall—

(MARCUS *rushes in, with* TRINA—*a lovely young woman— in tow.* MCTEAGUE *stares at her, speaking to* MARCUS.)

MCTEAGUE: I said—

MARCUS: She's bleedin', Mac.

MCTEAGUE: All right, all right…

(MCTEAGUE *gets out of the chair and motions to* TRINA, *who's frightened.*)

MCTEAGUE: Siddown.

(TRINA *sits.*)

MCTEAGUE: Where's the tooth?

(*She hands him the tooth.* MCTEAGUE *holds it up.*)

MARCUS: We run to the stop, and the trolley was crankin' away, and we thought we could hop it—

McTEAGUE: Open.

(TRINA *opens her mouth.* McTEAGUE *gives it a cursory look, then he steps away and pulls* MARCUS *aside.* TRINA *waits for* McTEAGUE *to come back, her mouth open.*)

McTEAGUE: *(To* MARCUS*)* Another dentist, a fancy gent, sports the most amazing vets, just set up shop—

MARCUS: What's wrong with *you*?

(Pause)

McTEAGUE: Mosta the women I see are older.

MARCUS: So?

McTEAGUE: Mosta the younger ones, like that, the ones that work at the soda-water fountain across the street, and the shops, they go to this other fellow...

MARCUS: So?

(Pause. McTEAGUE *can't explain his objection.)*

McTEAGUE: Tell her to come around tomorrow. I'll see what I can do.

MARCUS: Can't you tell her?

(Pause. McTEAGUE *turns to* TRINA, *whose mouth is still open.)*

McTEAGUE: Come back in the morning. I need the light.

(TRINA *nods, mouth open.* McTEAGUE *addresses* MARCUS*:*)

McTEAGUE: See what I mean?

MARCUS: About what?

McTEAGUE: You never know what they're up to. Why don't she close her mouth? *(To* TRINA*:)* Close yer mouth!

(Embarrassed, TRINA *does so.)*

TRINA: I'm tasting blood a little, still.

McTEAGUE: You couldn'ta said so? Open! *(He picks up a block of cotton and pulls off wisps, which he stuffs in* TRINA's *mouth. He looks at* MARCUS.*)* They never tell you anything. You always have to guess. You never know. *(Not paying attention to what he's doing, he stuffs* TRINA's *cheek with cotton.)*

(7)

(The dental parlor. Sunday)

*(*McTEAGUE *stands at his window with his concertina. It's late at night and he's still awake. He sings softly:)*

McTEAGUE:
"They soon reached the desert, where Betsy gave out,
And down in the sand she lay rolling about;
While Ike in great terror looked on in surprise,
Saying, Betsy, get up, you'll get sand in yer eyes."
(He stops. Something is bothering him, but he doesn't know what it is. He stares out into the night.)

(8)

(The dental parlor. Day)

*(*MISS BAKER *is in the chair. Behind her,* TRINA *waits her turn.)*

*(*McTEAGUE *is preparing his instruments and trying not to look at* TRINA.*)*

MISS BAKER: Say something, won't you, Doctor McTeague? I'm so nervous, I know it'll help if you'd natter away, 'bout anything, time and tide—

McTEAGUE: Open!

MISS BAKER: —the time of day, just the sound of a voice...

(For a second, she opens her mouth.)

McTEAGUE: Talk and work?

MISS BAKER: At the same time? Can you?

McTEAGUE: No.

(Pause. McTEAGUE *begins to examine* MISS BAKER *in silence.)*

MISS BAKER: Try?

(Pause. McTEAGUE *stops working, glancing at* TRINA.*)*

McTEAGUE: How's old Grannis?

MISS BAKER: Talk about something else.

*(*McTEAGUE *goes back to work for a moment, stops again.)*

McTEAGUE: I thought you two was sweet on the other.

MISS BAKER: By accident, our rooms adjoin. I've never met the man, in actual fact. *(Pause)* He's the youngest son of a baronet. Isn't that odd? And his stepfather wronged him cruelly.

*(*McTEAGUE *works for a second, stops.)*

McTEAGUE: I don't know if I buy all that.

MISS BAKER: I do. You have only to look at his hands.

McTEAGUE: His hands is all cat-clawed and dog-bit up.

MISS BAKER: But beneath the scars. Very distinguished and swell.

McTEAGUE: Why are you blushing?

MISS BAKER: I'm not. I'm flushed. You keep it like a furnace here. In fact, I'm feeling a little faint. In fact, I have to go.

(Jumping up from the chair, MISS BAKER *rushes out of the room.)*

*(*McTEAGUE, *embarrassed, looks at* TRINA.*)*

McTEAGUE: You know anybody who likes a dentist?

TRINA: People get used to the pain they're in. *(Pause)* Should I sit?

McTEAGUE: Might as well.

(TRINA gets into the chair.)

McTEAGUE: Let's have a look then. Better take off the lid.

(TRINA removes her hat, holding it in her lap, as McTEAGUE examines her mouth with a little mirror.)

(In its cage, McTEAGUE's canary begins to sing.)

McTEAGUE: Hmm…hmmmm…hmpf!…uh-huh… hmmm… *(Finishing up his examination, he steps away from the chair.)*

TRINA: It's a dreadful disfigurement, don't you think?

McTEAGUE: Not yet. Although—the tooth that's *next* to the one that's broke…

TRINA: What about it?

McTEAGUE: It's not gonna last. It has to come, too.

TRINA: No!

McTEAGUE: Excuse me?

TRINA: No! I wont have it!

McTEAGUE: It ain't exactly a case of you having a say…

TRINA: One hole in my smile is bad enough. But two…

(TRINA starts to cry. McTEAGUE is abashed.)

McTEAGUE: Please don't…

TRINA: I always liked my mouth the way it was.

McTEAGUE: I'm sure you did. It's a very—workable mouth. Even now. With one tooth gone. Another won't…and we all of us…time and tide, and our bodies end up, grass—

TRINA: But I'm young!

(Pause)

McTEAGUE: There's another dentist, two blocks up, poses a lot and rides a bicycle...

TRINA: And what would *he* say? Would he tell me to give up hope?

McTEAGUE: He'd say... *(He thinks hard.)* ...he could probably drill a socket, into the roots that was left, and sockets in the molar and cuspid, and partly if he bridged across it, and partly if he crowned, he could fill the gap. Be a bear of an operation, though. You'd have to come in for a couple of weeks. But you'd have the smile, when I was done, you always had.

TRINA: *(A question)* The other dentist would say this.

McTEAGUE: Yes.

TRINA: Would you?

(Pause)

McTEAGUE: I'd give it one hell of a shot.

TRINA: Then won't you start?

(Pause)

McTEAGUE: I can't talk and work.

TRINA: I'll listen to your bird.

(The canary trills on.)

(9)

(The dental parlor. Sunday.)

(McTEAGUE, in his chair, is softly playing the concertina.)

McTEAGUE:
"Did you ever hear tell of sweet Betsy from Pike..."
(He stops. Dissatisfied, he tries another song:)
"Oh the Ear-eye-ee was a-risin'..."

(He puts the concertina down. Then he takes a handkerchief out and unfolds it, uncovering TRINA's *tooth.)*

(As he holds the tooth up, TRINA *appears behind the chair.)*

TRINA: Open!

McTEAGUE: I can't sleep. *(Pause)* I got to sleep! *(Pause)* You ought to gone to that other dentist. The bicycle-rider.

TRINA: Somebody finer grained...

McTEAGUE: —than me. I got to keep touchin' yer face while I work, yer little chin, there's a vein in your eyelid flutters I want to still...and this smell comes offa yer hair...

TRINA: Spit!

McTEAGUE: I can't sleep. I got to sleep.

*(*TRINA *disappears.)*

*(*McTEAGUE *stares out.)*

(10)

(The dental parlor)

*(*McTEAGUE *is working on* TRINA, *across whose dress the dentist has thrown an apron. He stops.)*

McTEAGUE: I'm sorry.

TRINA: What?

McTEAGUE: A strand of your hair, got caught on my ring.

TRINA: It didn't hurt.

McTEAGUE: Well, that's fine.

TRINA: You worry too much about hurting me.

McTEAGUE: Do I?

TRINA: I'm not a china doll. I don't break.

McTEAGUE: I know…

TRINA: Then don't fret so much.

McTEAGUE: It's just, I *have* to hurt you some. I already have. Last week I could feel you holding your breath for an *hour*.

TRINA: I didn't mind.

McTEAGUE: I minded.

(Pause)

TRINA: You make me think of a joke I heard: Why are dentists always so gloomy?

McTEAGUE: Are we? I guess we are. I don't know.

TRINA: Because they're always looking down in the mouth.

(Pause. McTEAGUE laughs.)

McTEAGUE: "Down in the mouth." I just got it.

TRINA: That didn't take long.

McTEAGUE: I know one. Want me to tell it?

TRINA: Yes, please.

McTEAGUE: Well…a dentist says to his patient, "This drilling is gonna get worrisome, now. You want gas?" And the patient says, "I *got* gas, thanks. Musta been somethin I et!"

(TRINA laughs.)

McTEAGUE: Yeah. Well. The afternoon's slipping away.

TRINA: Resume your tortures, doctor.

(McTEAGUE bends over to work again.)

McTEAGUE: My mother had a bottle of scent like that…

TRINA: What scent?

MᴄTᴇᴀɢᴜᴇ: Yer perfume. I wondered what it was.

Tʀɪɴᴀ: I'm not wearing perfume.

(Pause)

MᴄTᴇᴀɢᴜᴇ: I beg your pardon.

Tʀɪɴᴀ: Not necessary.

(Embarrassed, MᴄTᴇᴀɢᴜᴇ *goes back to work.* Tʀɪɴᴀ *moans.)*

MᴄTᴇᴀɢᴜᴇ: Should I stop?

Tʀɪɴᴀ: No. Its all right. Go on.

*(*MᴄTᴇᴀɢᴜᴇ *continues to work.* Tʀɪɴᴀ *flinches.)*

MᴄTᴇᴀɢᴜᴇ: I know it's bad. Dont tell me it ain't.

Tʀɪɴᴀ: A little.

MᴄTᴇᴀɢᴜᴇ: It's gonna get worse. I could give you ether.

Tʀɪɴᴀ: What does it do?

MᴄTᴇᴀɢᴜᴇ: Just puts you to sleep.

(Pause)

Tʀɪɴᴀ: Maybe I better.

MᴄTᴇᴀɢᴜᴇ: It's nothing to be afraid of, I just…pour some onto this sponge, like so, and you breathe the fumes when I hold it under your nose, and count to ten, or as far as you get. Ready?

Tʀɪɴᴀ: I guess.

*(*MᴄTᴇᴀɢᴜᴇ *holds the ether-soaked sponge to her face.)*

MᴄTᴇᴀɢᴜᴇ: Count!

Tʀɪɴᴀ: One…two… hree… *(She goes slack in the chair, her head lolls.)*

*(*MᴄTᴇᴀɢᴜᴇ *props open* Tʀɪɴᴀ*'s mouth, preparing to pull a tooth. Then he steps back, staring at her. He closes her*

*mouth. Then he runs one trembling finger over her cheek.
With a visible effort of will, he pulls himself away.)*

MCTEAGUE: What am I doing?

*(Terrified of what he's feeling, MCTEAGU sits in one of the
waiting-chairs and stares at TRINA. Despite himself, he gets
up again and crosses to his unconscious patient. Leaning
over, he breathes her odor in. Again he pulls back. But he's
overwhelmed. Seizing her head in both his hands, he kisses
her full and hard on the mouth. Then he drops her back in
the chair and staggers away.)*

*(TRINA sits up. MCTEAGUE and TRINA share a dream. She
gets out of the chair.)*

TRINA: Your hands are so big.

MCTEAGUE: Alla me's big. *(Pause)* I don't know. I was a
car-boy. Up in the mines.

TRINA: Your hands don't make any sense.

MCTEAGUE: My head is big. *(Pause)* I ended a brawl
with my head, one time. Butted a guy through a door.
(Pause) Back a long time. *(Pause)* I don't fight anymore.

TRINA: Don't you get tired? Holding up that block?

MCTEAGUE: *(Agreeing)* Don't I? Oh… *(Pause)* Let me lay
it down…

TRINA: No.

MCTEAGUE: But let me.

TRINA: How would I breathe.

MCTEAGUE: I'd breathe.

TRINA: In me?

(Pause)

MCTEAGUE: Your hands don't make any sense. I could
snap your wrist like a stalk.

(Pause)

(TRINA *gets back in the chair. The dream is over; she sleeps again.*)

(MCTEAGUE *stares at her.*)

MCTEAGUE: What did I almost... Pull the tooth I was pulling, get her the hell... (*Forcing himself to be businesslike, he returns to the chair, picks up his forceps, and opens* TRINA's *mouth. He tries to pull the tooth with forceps. The tooth won't budge.*) Goddammit! (*He flips the forceps away, stares at her. Then, in a quick and determined way, he sticks his fingers in her mouth and pulls.*) Al...most... home. (*He steps back from the chair, holding the bloody tooth he's pulled.*)

(TRINA *stirs.* MCTEAGUE *uneasily hides the tooth in a pocket.*)

TRINA: Oh...I don't...where...

MCTEAGUE: Back in the land of the living.

TRINA: I had the most horrible dreams.

MCTEAGUE: The ether'll do that. Probably got a head-ache too.

TRINA: I do. I feel sick. Are you done?

MCTEAGUE: For now.

(MCTEAGUE *whisks the cover off* TRINA. *She starts to get up, he gently pushes her back.*)

MCTEAGUE: Miss Trina?

TRINA: What?

(MCTEAGUE *begins to stuff cotton into her cheek.*)

MCTEAGUE: I know this is sudden and all...

TRINA: Ih anna-hing wong?

MCTEAGUE: I hope not. See—I like you better than anyone else...

TRINA: Wha oo oo mee?

McTEAGUE: What's the matter with us getting married?

(TRINA *gets out of the chair, astonished, pushing*
McTEAGUE *aside.*)

McTEAGUE: Will you?

TRINA: Geh mah-hied? (*She starts for the door.*)

McTEAGUE: Won't you even consider it?

TRINA: I doe ee-huh know you! (*She pulls the cotton out
of her mouth and throws it away.*) I don't even know you!

(*As* TRINA *turns to flee, she runs right into the maid*
MARIA, *who blocks her way.*)

MARIA: Buy a lottery ticket?

TRINA: What??

MARIA: For a dollar only.

(MARIA *offers* TRINA *a lottery ticket.*)

McTEAGUE: Get goin', Maria. Those things are illegal.

MARIA: (*Blocking* TRINA's *exit*) Dudn't keep people from
winning, does it? Buying a palace on Telegraph Hill?

TRINA: (*Frantic to escape*) Will you—

MARIA: (*Not budging*) Bein' set up for the resta their
lives?

TRINA: Please!—

MARIA: —for a dollar?

TRINA: Oh, give me one. Hurry. Here.

(TRINA *thrusts a bill at* MARIA, *grabs a ticket, and pushes
past the maid.*)

(MARIA *calls out, as* TRINA *rushes off:*)

MARIA: You win?—you buy gold dishes. Keep `em safe
in a leather trunk. Raise the lid in the dark, the room
lights up, it does, I seen it.

(McTEAGUE *has taken* TRINA's *tooth from his pocket. He holds it in his palm.*)

MARIA: You got any junk?

McTEAGUE: *(Not really listening)* Go away, Miss Maraca.

(Seeing McTEAGUE *is distracted,* MARIA *picks up the forceps the dentist had dropped on the floor. Then she sidles up to the tray that holds the golden dental tape.)*

MARIA: The name is Maria Miranda *Macapa. (Pause; as if an afterthought:)* Had a flying squirrel and let him go.

McTEAGUE: So you told me. Many times. And also about the golden plates. Go away.

MARIA: The man I useta sell junk to died.

McTEAGUE: That'll happen.

(Without making a sound, MARIA *picks up the golden tape and pockets it, along with the forceps.)*

MARIA: I gotta find someone else.

McTEAGUE: So do I. Go away.

*(*MARIA *tiptoes away with her booty.* McTEAGUE *holds up the tooth.)*

McTEAGUE: Find someone else. Someone else... *(Pause)* I won't. *(Pause)* I WON'T! *(He kisses the tooth.)*

(11)

*(*ZERKOW's *junk shop.)*

*(*MARIA, *lugging her bulging pillowcase, is talking to the owner* ZERKOW, *a used-up miner who never hit it big.)*

MARIA: Give me a dollar. I dust your shop.

ZERKOW: A dollar?

MARIA: This dust is deep.

ZERKOW: I ain't never *had* a dollar.

MARIA: Ha!

ZERKOW: And also, this isn't a shop.

MARIA: Go ahead. Pull my *other* leg, then.

ZERKOW: Not at all. It's what you would call a museum.

MARIA: It's junk.

ZERKOW: And what's junk? Things that useta be useful, that's all. And now they ain't. So you sell 'em to me. And they go on display in the shadows here: the Museum of the No-Longer Useful.

MARIA: Doll with no head—I'd pay two bits to see one a those. A petrified owl that all the feathers fell out—

ZERKOW: I sell the feathers separate.

MARIA: Grease all over everything. Dust—

ZERKOW: —which comes from you gotta know where.

MARIA: Where?

ZERKOW: "Ashes to ashes…?"

(MARIA *considers what* ZERKOW*'s saying.*)

MARIA: I have to go.

ZERKOW: "Dust to dust?"

(*As* MARIA *tries to leave,* ZERKOW *grabs her arm.*)

ZERKOW: Wheres the dust come from?

MARIA: The dead. Let me go.

ZERKOW: You afraid of the dead?

MARIA: You ain't?

ZERKOW: That makes you afraid of everything that ever was. People and buildings and clothes and trees, kites and whales and baseball bats, little puppies that choke on a chicken-bone, mountains that get ground down to nothing, oceans—

MARIA: *Water* don't die!

ZERKOW: The Dead Sea? *(Pause)* You ever stay up till the cable stops?

MARIA: Who's asking?

ZERKOW: And just now and just then, all the other night-sounds will fade…

MARIA: But it's never completely still. There's another sound.

ZERKOW: Right! Even softer. Always there. Below it all. What is it?

(MARIA knows but shakes her head.)

ZERKOW: It's everything that ever was, going to dust. It's all the dust sifting down. Onto your food. Onto your lips, that kiss the dust off other lips. Makes us all museums.

MARIA: Why do you do this—make me afraid? I don't think you are nice. Let go of my hand.

ZERKOW: Just having the smallest fun. In the dark.

(MARIA moves away.)

ZERKOW: I thought you come in to sell me somethin'.

(MARIA stops.)

MARIA: Oh. You like gold?

ZERKOW: I used to be a miner, once. I guess that don't answer your question, exactly—

MARIA: I useta be a launder-lady. Don't mean I like clean sheets. Just a job.

ZERKOW: It wasn't a job. It was more in the way of an avocation. Worked myself till my health gave out. One time I didn't sleep for seven months.

MARIA: Never panned out?

ZERKOW: Look around.

MARIA: I'm looking. Now *you* look.

(MARIA *opens her hand, revealing some of* McTEAGUE's *gold dental tape.*)

ZERKOW: What is it?

MARIA: It's gold for teeth.

ZERKOW: I'll buy it.

MARIA: How much?

ZERKOW: Whatever you're askin'. Sell it to me. Evrything else I have. But I don't have gold.

MARIA: I know.

ZERKOW: Name your price.

(*Pause*)

MARIA: I don't think so. Not today.

(*Pause*)

ZERKOW: Then why'd you come in?

MARIA: Just having some fun. In the dark.

(ZERKOW, *furious, watches her walk away.*)

(12)

(*A swanky neighborhood. Late afternoon.*)

(TRINA's *waiting for* MARCUS, *who's just delivered a dog to a fancy address. She looks around her in wonder, calling out to the offstage* MARCUS.)

TRINA: All this block is somebody's home?

MARCUS: (*Off*) You should see the doghouse. (*He enters, leash in hand.*) Got a little more room than my flat.

TRINA: What's it like inside?

MARCUS: Well, it's full of bones, and slobber and hair—

TRINA: Not the kennel! —the *mansion*!

MARCUS: I walk their invalid hound. They don't take me on tours.

TRINA: *(Of the house, trying not to be envious)* Maybe you'd rattle around.

MARCUS: You might not mind bein' rattled. Let's go.

(But TRINA *lingers, staring at the house.)*

TRINA: My father thought, if he never stopped working—all his life, not even to breathe—he'd live in a house like that someday.

MARCUS: Tell him to work on oppressin' his fellows. That's the way you want to rustle.

TRINA: We keep on movin' to smaller and smaller bungalows.

MARCUS: Starvin'?

TRINA: Not yet.

MARCUS: Then go on to yerself. Ya wanta stop by and see Mac?

TRINA: I *don't.*

MARCUS: He drill you too hard or what's yer problem?

TRINA: I'm late for my ferry. Come on.

*(*MARCUS *and* TRINA *exit.)*

(From the opposite side, MCTEAGUE *enters. He's been following* MARCUS *and* TRINA. *Now he watches them amble off.)*

MCTEAGUE: Yer hurting me. *(Pause)* Yer HURTING ME!

(While he stares at his love and his rival, the FANCY DENTIST *bicycles past, almost running down* MCTEAGUE.)*

FANCY DENTIST: Watch your back!

(The FANCY DENTIST *is gone. Angrily,* MCTEAGUE *calls after:)*

McTEAGUE: Ain't you that fancy other fellow? *I* could ride a bicycle. Well? I could wear a pink vest! You can't make small of me, you little—pup! I'll thump your head. *(He stands in front of the millionaire's palace and fumes.)*

(13)

(Cliff House, near the water)

(McTEAGUE and MARCUS—who's had a few beers—have wandered out of the tavern, up to the cliff.)

MARCUS: It's capitalists that's wreckin' the cause of labor, white-livered drones, with their livers white as snow, eatin' the bread of widows and orphans… That's where the evil lies. Right?

McTEAGUE: *(Distracted)* That's it. I think it's their livers.

MARCUS: Ain't it time for this fog to burn off? Where the hell are the dogs? Nice animals, ain't they? Go inside for a single beer, the dogs depart. You think that yelpin's them? Or seals?

(McTEAGUE, lost in thought, doesn't answer.)

MARCUS: Mac?

McTEAGUE: What's that?

MARCUS: You heard a single word I said? What's the matter with you? You got a bean about somethin'? Huh? Spit it out.

McTEAGUE: I don't. It's nothin'…no.

MARCUS: I guess yer in love, then.

McTEAGUE: What??

MARCUS: Well somethin's biting you, anyhow. Has any duck been doing you dirt?

McTEAGUE: No…

MARCUS: But ain't we pals? Better tell me what's up. I'll do what I can to help ya.

(Pause)

MCTEAGUE: It's—it's Miss Sieppe.

MARCUS: My cousin Trina? How do you mean?

MCTEAGUE: I, I—I don't know...

MARCUS: You mean...that you, too... *(He is stunned.)*

MCTEAGUE: I can't help it. It ain't my fault, I swear it aint. She'd come to my parlor, three or four times a week, and I'd have to touch her lips, and her chin—

MARCUS: I'm fond of her chin myself. And the way her forehead shines. And the smell of her hair.

MCTEAGUE: And her breath—

MARCUS: What about it?

MCTEAGUE: Don't you know? It's sweet, and, well, and—

MARCUS: Warm.

MCTEAGUE: But ain't it? Makes you...

MARCUS: What?

MCTEAGUE: I can't say, exactly—wanta get closer—

MARCUS: How close?

MCTEAGUE: Don't you know?

MARCUS: I know a lotta those things, remember? We're talking about my girl.

MCTEAGUE: I heard you was seein' a coupla others.

MARCUS: And what if I was? You want them, too?

(Pause)

MCTEAGUE: All this, it came on so slow that I, it was done before I could help myself. You brought her to me—

MARCUS: —as a patient, Mac. Not a gift.

McTEAGUE: I can't think of anything else, night and day. It's everything. It's everything. *(Pause) You* said she wasn't rich enough.

MARCUS: She might have been. I might have been.

McTEAGUE: But I'd marry her *now*. Would you?

(Pause)

MARCUS: Have you told her how you feel?

McTEAGUE: *(Nodding)* She ran away.

(Pause)

MARCUS: So what are we gonna do about this?

McTEAGUE: I don't want it to come between you and me—

MARCUS: Well it has to, don't it?

McTEAGUE: I guess it does.

MARCUS: Unless I give her up.

(Pause)

McTEAGUE: I couldn't ask you to do that.

MARCUS: No? What the hell do you think you *been* doing?

McTEAGUE: I can't explain. It's just everything.

MARCUS: Then how can I stand in your way?

(Pause)

McTEAGUE: I never had a pal like you—

MARCUS: —but you want her as bad as all that.

McTEAGUE: Like I'm choking to death. And she was air.

MARCUS: I'll pull out. I'll give her up. To you, old man.

(McTEAGUE, *dumbfounded, pumps* MARCUS *hand.)*

McTEAGUE: I *never* had a pal like you.

(MARCUS *turns away with a heavy sigh.*)

McTEAGUE: But you got this hang-dog look—

MARCUS: I ain't sayin my heart ain't broke.

McTEAGUE: Oh, Mark—

MARCUS: *(Choking up at the thought of his own self-sacrifice)* —but that ain't the same as sore. I want you to be as happy as... well, as happy as I might have been. I forgive you. More—I forgive you freely.

McTEAGUE: Who was those friends in the Bible? Damon and Pythias?

MARCUS: Something like that... And I'll take you out to her house next week.

McTEAGUE: I can't go to her house! She *ran* from me.

MARCUS: She ran as far as her house. So hunt her down.

(Pause)

McTEAGUE: I dreamed about the two of us, her and me, swimming out to the rock. The one like a giant tooth, all shining?

MARCUS: What did you do when you got there?

(Pause)

McTEAGUE: I don't remember.

(Pause. Offstage, two dogs begin to bark ferociously.)

MARCUS: The dogs're back. Hey, dogs.

McTEAGUE: You think they oughta be fightin' like that?

MARCUS: Sheba! Cornelius! Chew each other's ankles! Good dogs!

McTEAGUE: Ain't they gettin too close to the edge of the cliff?

MARCUS: Not yet. *Some* day. All rolled up in a ball of snarlin' fur. Over they'll go.

(14)

(The salt flats outside of Oakland)

(TRINA wanders in with her MOTHER, a German woman who came to the country a few years back with her family. (TRINA carries a picnic hamper. MOTHER holds her hand to her eyes, against the glare, and looks out.)

MOTHER: I don't get—your father and Marcus, look, where the tide is out: They are shooting at clams.

(TRINA laughs, shaking her head.)

MOTHER: Then what do they pop?

TRINA: Tin cans.

MOTHER: And the other? The one who stands with his hands, so big, in his pockets?

TRINA: He's just a friend of Marcus. I told you.

MOTHER: Then why does he stare at you so?

(Pause)

TRINA: I'm very grateful he fixed my teeth. But his head is too big. His hands are, too. And he doesn't bathe nearly often enough. Or wash his clothes. Or clean his room. Or think about things. Or speak.

(Pause)

MOTHER: Then why do you want to touch him?

TRINA: Mother!

MOTHER: Don't touch him, then. I go to find a facility. Also, he comes.

(MOTHER points at MCTEAGUE, who's entering.)

TRINA: *(As MOTHER starts to exit)* Don't leave me here!

(TRINA's MOTHER *pushes her back.*)

MOTHER: I think you stay. Better you learn your mind.

(MOTHER *exits in one direction as* MCTEAGUE *enters in another.*)

(*For a moment* MCTEAGUE *and* TRINA *just stand, apart, not talking.*)

MCTEAGUE: Fine day for a picnic, ain't it? There ain't a cloud.

TRINA: That's so. Oh wait—there's one, just over Telegraph Hill.

MCTEAGUE: That's smoke.

TRINA: It's a cloud. Smoke isn't white that way.

(MCTEAGUE *stares.*)

MCTEAGUE: You're right. It's a cloud.

TRINA: I knew it was. I never say a thing unless I'm sure.

(*Pause*)

MCTEAGUE: Are you mad at me, still?

TRINA: You just frightened me.

MCTEAGUE: That wasn't what I meant to do.

TRINA: I know. It's all right. It's forgotten.

MCTEAGUE: Except, I don't want it forgotten—

TRINA: Except, I do.

(*Just then* MARCUS *enters, nattily dressed in a hunting jacket and brandishing a rifle.*)

(*Welcoming the interruption,* TRINA *moves away from* MCTEAGUE *and starts to set out the picnic.*)

TRINA: Is target practice over?

MARCUS: The tide's comin in. And I'm rusty.

TRINA: Mama thought you were stalking clams.

MARCUS: Hit more of them than cans, I bet.

(MARCUS *pulls* McTEAGUE *aside.*)

MARCUS: How rusty are *you*?

McTEAGUE: (*Shaking his head in defeat*) Don't leave us alone again.

MARCUS: She won't tumble?

(McTEAGUE *shakes his head.* MARCUS *looks at* TRINA, *who's opening up a bottle.*)

MARCUS: Maybe the beer'll help.

McTEAGUE: I ain't waitin' that long. I'm headin back.

MARCUS: But she likes you, Mac.

McTEAGUE: Says who?

MARCUS: Is she running away? Is she screaming at you?

McTEAGUE: That ain't a whole lot of a recommendation.

MARCUS: Just think of her as a china shop. And you're the bull with a problem. Solution? Go extremely slow.

(TRINA *pulls a roasted chicken out of the hamper.*)

TRINA: (*Calling to them*) If anyone's hungry...

McTEAGUE: *I* am.

MARCUS: (*Whispered*) No you ain't. Watchin' you eat a chicken bare-handed is not a pretty sight.

McTEAGUE: What's wrong with the way I eat?

(TRINA's MOTHER *reenters.*)

MOTHER: (*Looking off*) They put the boat in the water now. Your brother whines, your father barks, I don't watch.

TRINA: Where? ·

MOTHER: I don't watch!

MARCUS: *(Pointing off)* Is that them?

(TRINA comes down to join MCTEAGUE and MARCUS.)

TRINA: It's a little toy steamboat—just this big—and it runs with an alcohol lamp—

MOTHER: —they say. They only try it out today.

MARCUS: So this is the maiden voyage.

MOTHER: Chicken leg, Doctor McTeague?

MCTEAGUE: I wouldn't say no.

MARCUS: *(Under his breath)* Yes, you would.

MCTEAGUE: I mean—no. No, thank you.

TRINA: *(Pointing out)* Look!

MOTHER: *(Hurrying over to look)* Ca-TAS-trophe!

MARCUS: The boiler blew.

MCTEAGUE: It's sinking.

MOTHER: Your brother cries, your father shakes him up, I don't watch—

TRINA: But maybe you better, Mama—

MOTHER: *(Calling off)* Herman! The blood goes to his head, you hold him that way. Marcus, help me to rescue your cousin—

(MOTHER and MARCUS run off.)

MOTHER: Herman! With the upside down, now, HALT!

(They're gone. MCTEAGUE and TRINA are left alone again.)

MCTEAGUE: Don't you wanta go down there?

TRINA: No.

MCTEAGUE: Do you want me to leave you be?

(TRINA doesn't answer.)

MCTEAGUE: The boat's going down.

TRINA: Where?

McTEAGUE: There. It's gone. Just bubbles.

TRINA: Poor little kid.

McTEAGUE: If I had enough money, I'd buy him another.

TRINA: *(Touched)* Would you?

(Far off a train whistle blows.)

McTEAGUE: That's the Sacramento train.

TRINA: I know a girl in Sacramento.

McTEAGUE: I was in Sacramento once. Eight years ago.

TRINA: Is it as nice as San Francisco?

McTEAGUE: It's hot. I practiced there for a while.

TRINA: Were you happy?

McTEAGUE: I thought I was. I didn't know.

TRINA: What?

McTEAGUE: That I could be happier, maybe.

(Pause)

TRINA: Don't you love the ocean?

McTEAGUE: I guess.

TRINA: I'd like to go off in one of those great big sailing ships. Just away and away and away…

McTEAGUE: Where?

TRINA: Anywhere. If I had enough money, I would.

(Pause)

McTEAGUE: If I had enough money, I'd buy a big gilded tooth for a sign. Hanging outside my window.

TRINA: And you'd buy my brother a boat.

McTEAGUE: And I'd buy you a ring.

TRINA: Don't TALK like that!

MCTEAGUE: Just say you don't like me. Say it! I'll go away.

TRINA: *(Not able to say it)* I don't—...

MCTEAGUE: Say it.

TRINA: I can't...

MCTEAGUE: SAY IT.

TRINA: Your head is too big! Your hands are, too! You don't bathe or clean your clothes. Or your room. And your breath—

MCTEAGUE: What about it?

TRINA: It's hot. And your skin—

MCTEAGUE: What about it?

TRINA: What does it feel like?

MCTEAGUE: Skin.

TRINA: And your heart—

MCTEAGUE: What about it?

TRINA: It's *loud*—

MCTEAGUE: You can't hear my heart—

TRINA: I can—like thunder—

MCTEAGUE: That isn't my heart. It's yours.

TRINA: No!

MCTEAGUE: For the last time: Say you don't like me. SAY it!

TRINA: I—don't— *(She can't finish.)*

(Suddenly, MCTEAGUE grabs TRINA, pressing her tightly against him.)

TRINA: Please—

MCTEAGUE: No.

(McTEAGUE *holds* TRINA *tight; she struggles in vain to free herself. Then she stops her struggle. She turns her face to his. They kiss each other full and hard on the mouth.*)

(A train roars by.)

(McTEAGUE *and* TRINA *break their embrace.*)

TRINA: You don't understand—

(McTEAGUE *kisses* TRINA *hard, again. She kisses him back.*)

(Unnoticed by the lovers, MARCUS *enters and watches them, unseen.*)

(McTEAGUE *and* TRINA *finally break their embrace.*)

TRINA: Wait a minute. You don't understand. I don't love you.

McTEAGUE: Yer lying.

(Pause)

TRINA: I am. Oh, my lord. I am. *(She backs away from* McTEAGUE.*)*

McTEAGUE: Let me kiss you again.

TRINA: No…

McTEAGUE: But you love me. Don't lie.

(Pause)

TRINA: I love you.

(TRINA *runs off, still not seeing* MARCUS. McTEAGUE *watches her go.*)

McTEAGUE: I got her, by God. I *got* her!

(MARCUS *steps forward.*)

MARCUS: Now you just got to keep her.

(McTEAGUE *is more startled by* MARCUS's *statement than his presence.*)

McTEAGUE: How?

MARCUS: Maybe sprinkle a little salt on her tail.

McTEAGUE: No—how?

MARCUS: Well, wine her and dine her. Be nice to her horrible family. Buy her junk.

McTEAGUE: Why can't I just drag her off someplace?

MARCUS: Where?

McTEAGUE: You know how quiet Sunday used to be? Some place like that. It's always Sunday somewhere on the earth. I heard that once.

MARCUS: Not Sunday. Night. It's always *night*, ya big gorilla—

(At this moment the FANCY DENTIST *bicycles past, almost colliding with* MARCUS.)

FANCY DENTIST: Watch your back!

(The FANCY DENTIST *exits.)*

MARCUS: Watch my back?

McTEAGUE: *(In a daze)* That was him…

MARCUS: He say watch *my* back? Ain't I got a right to cross a street even, without they should mow me down?

McTEAGUE: That's the other dentist. The one with the carriage trade…

MARCUS: Well, tell him to watch *his* back, he don't want to find a knife in it…

McTEAGUE: Dudn't Trina deserve somebody like him? Turned out like that and educated? *He'd* know how to romance a girl.

MARCUS: Then why ain't he ridin a bicycle built for *two*?

*(*McTEAGUE *doesn't have an answer for this.)*

MARCUS: Exactly. *(He starts to exit.)* Come on,
Lochinvar. We got to get you some evenin' duds. *(He
exits.)*

*(Far off, the train that had roared past earlier whistles
again.)*

*(MCTEAGUE holds back a moment, overwhelmed by
everything that's happening.)*

(He listens to the faraway train disappear in the night.)

(15)

(Outside MCTEAGUE's apartment-building. Night)

*(MARIA sits on the steps of the building, as ZERKOW enters.
He sits beside her.)*

MARIA: You take the night air? I think you stay always
inside. In your den. Like a spider.

ZERKOW: Sometimes I go out. I heard a story 'bout you.

MARIA: What story?

ZERKOW: About a service of gold?

MARIA: What of it?

ZERKOW: You useta be rich?

MARIA: My family. Then, they wasn't. Long ago.

ZERKOW: And you had a service of golden dishes.

MARIA: What if we did?

ZERKOW: Well, don't you like to talk about it?

*(In the distance a fire-bell starts to clang, in rhythmical
bursts—1, 4, 3—like Morse code. MARIA and ZERKOW
don't notice, at first.)*

MARIA: I don't. It makes me sad. *(Pause)* There was
more than a hundred pieces—plates an' platters an'
soup tureens—an' all of em gold. In a leather trunk.

When you opened the lid, in the dark, it was like a pool when the sun shines down...

(MARIA *comes out of her reverie—to* ZERKOW's *dismay— when she sees* GRANNIS, *an elderly man, approaching.*)

(GRANNIS, *who has been silently counting the fire alarms, greets* MARIA.)

GRANNIS: Maria.

MARIA: Evenin', Mister Grannis.

ZERKOW: (*Trying to get* MARIA *back to the story*) Go on. "Like a pool with the light shinin' down..."

(GRANNIS *takes out a small card and consults it.* MARIA, *to get* ZERKOW's *goat, keeps talking to* GRANNIS.)

MARIA: Where's the fire?

GRANNIS: (*Referring to the card*) 1, 4, 3. Thats Grant and Folsom. (*He looks off, in search of the fire.*)

MARIA: Far off. We escape.

ZERKOW: 'less the wind shifts.

MARIA: An' our skin bubbles off. An' our bones turn black. Go chase yerself.

GRANNIS: I think I can see the glare...

(*Watching the glow, not looking at where he's going,* GRANNIS *bumps into* MISS BAKER, *who's entered from the opposite side. Her market basket falls to the stage, and a fish and a cabbage fall out. The cabbage rolls away. The two old people are mortified.*)

(*Unnoticed in the confusion,* MARCUS *appears in back and watches the scene.*)

GRANNIS: Oh, I'm terribly sorry, I—here, let me help you—

MISS BAKER: No, please, it's all right, I can manage, I— PLEASE. *Don't pick up my fish.*

(GRANNIS *stands up, embarrassed.*)

GRANNIS: I beg your pardon.

MISS BAKER: The odor, I mean, on your hands, you
needn't—

GRANNIS: Allow me at least to retrieve your cabbage.

(*As* MISS BAKER *recovers her fish and* GRANNIS *hunts
for the rolled-away cabbage,* MARIA *points them out to*
ZERKOW.)

MARIA: They love each other. Those two old birds.
Both of em sit up, late at night, him on his side of the
wall, and her on hers, and he binds his little books, and
she drinks her tea, and they keep each other company.

ZERKOW: (*Doubtful*) Have they met?

MARIA: That was it. Just now.

(GRANNIS *offers* MISS BAKER *the cabbage, which she takes
with trembling hands.*)

MARIA: (*Calling out, cont'd*) Cabbage and fish? The
building smells like a Polish wedding tonight.

(MISS BAKER *frantically exits, followed more slowly by*
GRANNIS.)

ZERKOW: *I'm* Polish.

MARIA: I'm Mexican. What you call "greaser".
"Chileño." So?

(MARCUS *moves in to stir things up.*)

MARCUS: So maybe you two outsiders should ought
to give comfort to one another. `stead of tearing each
other's jugulars out. Which sorta carnage warms the
owners hearts.

MARIA: You call me a greaser yourself. I hear you.

MARCUS: Maybe I'll be an owner someday. It's practice.

(A nattily dressed little man, the LOTTERY AGENT, *has entered. He interrupts.)*

LOTTERY AGENT: Excuse me, Im trying to find a Miss Trina Sieppe—

MARCUS: I'm her cousin, and former fi-ancy. State yer business, pal.

LOTTERY AGENT: Did she purchase a lottery ticket at this address?

MARCUS: Who's askin'?

MARIA: Sure she did. I sold it. Right in the doctor's parlors.

MARCUS: You the police?

LOTTERY AGENT: I'm not.

MARCUS: Care to tell us who you are?

LOTTERY AGENT: I don't. *(Pause)* It's urgent I find Miss Sieppe tonight—

MARCUS: We can't help you, jack—

MARIA: *(To* MARCUS*)* You know where she is. At the Orpheum show. And she comes back here.

LOTTERY AGENT: Then I'll wait.

MARCUS: Then—seeing as how I don't like your looks— I guess I ain't budging either.

(Pause. MARCUS *and the* LOTTERY AGENT *face off and wait.* ZERKOW *goes back to his new obsession.)*

ZERKOW: *(To* MARIA*)* You were saying? About the dishes?

MARIA: I already told you.

ZERKOW: Tell it again. *(Prompting her:)* "There was more than a hundred pieces…"

MARIA: …and all of em gold…

(16)

(At the theater)

(MCTEAGUE, TRINA, and TRINA's MOTHER watch the show, entranced. MCTEAGUE is wearing ill-fitting fancy dress.)

(A naughty singer is finishing off a number.)

SINGER: *(Off)* "Mademoiselle, I love you well,
I fain would kiss your toe.
Ah! Oui, monsieur, my cheeks are near,
you need not stoop so low.
Ah! Oui, monsieur, my cheeks are near,
you need not stoop so low."

(MCTEAGUE and his party applaud.)

MOTHER: Does she mean what I hope she doesn't?

TRINA: It's just a song.

(TRINA's MOTHER starts to get up.)

MOTHER: I go to find a facility.

(TRINA pulls her back in her seat.)

TRINA: Mama! The show isn't over!

MCTEAGUE: *(Low, confidential to TRINA)* I shouldn'ta bought her the lemonade.

TRINA: You shouldn't have bought us all these things. Tamales and peanuts and drinks, and the show—

MCTEAGUE: Are you happy?

TRINA: In heaven!

MCTEAGUE: I'd buy you the whole the-ay-ter.

TRINA: Oh, Mac… *(She gives his arm a squeeze.)*

(As she does, the flickering light of an early movie bathes them.)

MOTHER: What is this?

TRINA: The kinetescope, Mama. Oh! *(Pointing at the offstage screen:)* The horse is moving his head! Look!

McTEAGUE: My god—you could touch him…

MOTHER: *(Unsettled)* It's all a trick.

TRINA: Well, of course it's a trick. That's part of the fun.

MOTHER: A cable car comes on the stage? It does not.

TRINA: Then why is it headin' toward us, mama?

(TRINA's MOTHER stares at the screen in horror. TRINA nestles against McTEAGUE, who happily puts an arm around her.)

MOTHER: *Gott in Himmel!* —Get out of the way! *Get out of the way!*

(The kinetescope ends. TRINA laughs at her mother.)

TRINA: "It's all a trick?"

MOTHER: *(Getting up, mortified)* Is too *late* to find a facility. *(She rushes off, and we hear her loud mutter:)* Ca-TAS-trophe!

(McTEAGUE and TRINA are left alone.)

McTEAGUE: You want to go help her?

TRINA: No, I don't. I want to stay right where I am. Forever.

McTEAGUE: What was your favorite part?

TRINA: I liked it all. But maybe the man who played "Nearer My God To Thee" on the bottles of beer.

McTEAGUE: That was a corker, all right.

TRINA: What was yours?

McTEAGUE: When the magic lantern cable car was about in our laps. And you was afraid. And you leaned against me. Didn't you want me close?

TRINA: Yes.

McTEAGUE: I wanta stay close. Will you let me?

TRINA: Yes. *(She stares at him.)* What a funny nose you've got.

McTEAGUE: Funny how?

TRINA: All full of hair inside.

McTEAGUE: I never inspected it up that close.

TRINA: Do you know about the bald spot?

McTEAGUE: Where?

TRINA: Right on the top of your head. Bend over. *(He does. She kisses his head.)* That'll make the hair grow.

McTEAGUE: Trina?

TRINA: Old bear...

McTEAGUE: What's the good of waitin much longer? Why don't we get married?

TRINA: *No.*

McTEAGUE: Don't you like me well enough?

TRINA: Yes.

McTEAGUE: Then why not?

TRINA: Do you have any money saved?

McTEAGUE: Not yet.

TRINA: Well then...of the money you make, when you've paid all the bills at the end of the month—how much is left over?

McTEAGUE: Not any.

TRINA: Then how would we live?

(Pause)

McTEAGUE: You could work.

TRINA: I already do. I carve little Noah's arks for a store my Uncle Oelberman owns.

MCTEAGUE: How much does that make you?

TRINA: Three or four dollars a week. Not enough.

MCTEAGUE: Close, though.

TRINA: I could tell you what happens with close.

MCTEAGUE: What happens?

TRINA: We useta have neighbors, across the street. This dear old couple who lived on a pension. It wasn't enough to get by. It was close. One day they didn't come out of their house. And then a week passed. And then there was a smell. So my father broke in. And all he found, besides them, was a skeleton, maybe as big as your hand. Like a rat's.

MCTEAGUE: Trina!

TRINA: And either the rat was their very last meal, or maybe it starved to death, too. *(Pause)* Their pension wasn't enough. It was close.

(Pause)

MCTEAGUE: Things could get bad—

TRINA: When don't they, Mac?

MCTEAGUE: I wouldn't let you starve.

TRINA: How would you stop me?

(Pause. MCTEAGUE looks out at the theater.)

MCTEAGUE: I wish they'd start that magic lantern again.

TRINA: What for?

MCTEAGUE: I'd get you onto that trolley car. We'd ride away.

TRINA: Wed be done for, though, when the lights came up.

MCTEAGUE: We'd be gone. We'd never know.

(17)

(The dental parlor. Night.)

*(*TRINA's MOTHER *warily enters, followed by a blissful* McTEAGUE *and* TRINA*.)*

MOTHER: I don't know if I sleep so good. In here. Where so many teeth have died.

TRINA: It's a dental parlor, Mama. It's not a Chamber of Horrors.

MOTHER: No? But always—on the street, you walk by—you can hear the people. Screaming.

TRINA: It hurts Mac more than it hurts his patients, Mama, he's got such a great big heart—

McTEAGUE: *(Not sure* TRINA's *right about the hurting part)* Well—

MOTHER: *(Agreeing with* TRINA*)* This is so. *(To* McTEAGUE*:)* You and Marcus give us your rooms and then where do *you* sleep?

McTEAGUE: Old Grannis—the vet—has a room in his clinic.

TRINA: It *is* kind of you to let us stay over. We always have to leave things early—to catch the last boat. We'd have missed the kinetescope show.

MOTHER: *(Still disgruntled about her accident)* Such a trick to have missed!

McTEAGUE: Well, I guess I should leave you ladies be. I changed the sheets. There's a...water closet, end of the hall. And Marcus's room is right above us. *(To* TRINA*:)* Maybe that's where your mother'd rather sleep—

LOTTERY AGENT: *(Interrupting)* Miss Sieppe?

(They all turn and see the LOTTERY AGENT. *Behind him are* MARCUS, MARIA, MISS BAKER, *and* ZERKOW, *all about to bust a button.* TRINA *is taken aback.)*

TRINA: Yes?

LOTTERY AGENT: Miss Trina Sieppe?

TRINA: That's me. What is it?

LOTTERY AGENT: Miss Trina Sieppe of 1850 Mission Street in Oakland—

TRINA: *Yes.* Is something wrong?

MARIA: *(To the* LOTTERY AGENT*)* Will you get to the point?

TRINA: What *is* the point?

LOTTERY AGENT: The point, Miss Sieppe, as a matter of fact—

MARIA: *(Rushing in)* You just win five thousand dollars!

(MARIA *and her entourage applaud.)*

(TRINA *is stunned. The applause dies down.)*

TRINA: What?

MARIA: The lottery ticket I sell you wins!

LOTTERY AGENT: If your number *is* four hundred thousand and twelve…

TRINA: Yes, four—three oughts—and a twelve, I remember.

LOTTERY AGENT: Your number will have to be verified. But there's hardly a chance of error, Miss Sieppe. I congratulate you. You've won five thousand dollars.

(More applause)

TRINA: But I couldn't have.

LOTTERY AGENT: Why ever not?

TRINA: Why should *I* win?

LOTTERY AGENT: Why shouldn't you?

TRINA: But I haven't earned it. I don't deserve it.

LOTTERY AGENT: Believe me when I say, Miss Sieppe, that nobody ever does. It just happens. Lightning strikes and the landscape changes. Some are borne down, and others up. And why not you as soon as the next?

(Pause)

TRINA: I've won? *(Pause)* Oh, I've won, I've won, I've won, oh, momma, I've won five thousand dollars!

MOTHER: Kiss me, then. Before you forget who I am.

TRINA: Oh, momma.

(TRINA kisses her MOTHER as the others applaud.)

MOTHER: Whatever will you do with the money?

(Pause)

MARCUS: Get married on it, for one thing.

(Everyone cheers and whistles. MCTEAGUE and TRINA look at each other and blush.)

MARCUS: Talk about luck... Well ain't we gonna celebrate, dammit? Ain't every day you win five thousand dollars. No. It's only Sundays and legal holidays.

(MARCUS's jest cracks everyone up. He begins to pass out glasses.)

MARCUS: Old Frenna sent up what he likes to call bubble-water, with lotsa compliments. Where's Mister Grannis?

MARIA: I bet he sews his little books.

MISS BAKER: No, not at this hour—... *(Embarrassed at having spoken, she stops.)*

MARCUS: Go bring him down, Maria.

MISS BAKER: I hardly think you'd better. He doesn't indulge.

MARCUS: Indulges in autumn romances, don't he?

(MISS BAKER *blushes.* MARIA *runs off, as* MARCUS *pops the cork on a champagne bottle.* TRINA *screams at the sound of the pop.)*

MOTHER: *Ach du lieber—*

MARCUS: Ladies, don't need to get scairt, it ain't loaded.

(MARCUS *pours champagne as everyone laughs.)*

LOTTERY AGENT: I think I should say a few words.

(Cries of "Hear! Hear!")

LOTTERY AGENT: Its been my duty, my *cheerful* duty, to call upon winners of prizes as large as this, and offer the company's deepest felicitations. I have, in my experience, called upon many such: but never have I seen fortune so happily showered down as in this case.

(The crowd cheers.)

LOTTERY AGENT: I toast the prospective bride and groom, happy in their unexpected possession of a snug little fortune, and happier still in their unexpected possession of each other.

MARCUS: Outa sight! Outa sight!

(Everyone drinks. MCTEAGUE *smacks his lips, delighted.)*

MCTEAGUE: That's the best beer *I* ever drank!

(A pause—then the crowd cracks up. MCTEAGUE *is puzzled.)*

MCTEAGUE: Well, ain't it?

TRINA: *(Low)* It isn't beer. It's champagne.

(Pause)

MCTEAGUE: I knew that.

(MARIA *enters with* GRANNIS, *who's looking disheveled, as if he were just about to go to bed.)*

MARCUS: An' here's old Grannis! Get him a glass, Miss Baker.

MISS BAKER: I don't even *know* him!

MARCUS: Enough is enough, you two old birds. You been livin' side by side for years, it's time you two got acquainted at last. Miss Baker, this here is Mister Grannis. Mister Grannis, this is Miss Baker.

(The two old people stare at each other, shy as children.)

(MARCUS hands GRANNIS a glass of champagne.)

MARCUS: Toast each other's old age, why don't you, and have a sip of the swellest beer Mac's ever had.

(People laugh again; MCTEAGUE frowns.)

TRINA: Marcus, leave him alone. He knew it wasn't beer. He was making a joke.

MARCUS: Tryin' ta entertain us? In that case, he should make a speech.

(The crowd cries out: "Speech! Speech!")

MCTEAGUE: No. No speech!

MARCUS: You ought to do it, Mac. It's the proper caper.

MCTEAGUE: I don't know what to say.

MARCUS: Say somethin'. You *got* to.

(More cries of "Speech! Speech!")

(Reluctantly, MCTEAGUE takes center stage.)

MCTEAGUE: I ain't never made a speech before. But I'm glad Trina's won the prize—

MARCUS: I'll *bet* you are.

MCTEAGUE: —and I want to say that you're welcome, and drink a lot, and I'm much obliged to the lottery agent. Trina and I are gonna be married...and I'm glad everybody's here tonight, an' drink a lot, and I—an'—an'— That's— about all—I—gotta—say.

(Tumultuous applause. As well-wishers gather around
MCTEAGUE *and* TRINA, MARIA *follows* ZERKOW, *who's*
wandering off.)

MARIA: You clap an' smile an' cheer—

ZERKOW: I do.

MARIA: An' it's all like a knife in your heart.

*(*ZERKOW *stares at* MARIA.)*

ZERKOW: How do you know?

MARIA: I lose things too.

ZERKOW: Five thousand dollars…

MARIA: Bright heavy pieces…

ZERKOW: For nothing. For buying a ticket.

MARIA: *You* coulda bought a ticket.

ZERKOW: I didn't. You could've kept the golden dishes.

MARIA: I didn't.

ZERKOW: At least you had hold of em once, in your
hands—

MARIA: Bright as a sunset—

ZERKOW: And didn't you say they was hard to lift?
That heavy? Rang like a bell?

MARIA: Gone for good.

(Pause)

ZERKOW: Come back to my shack.

MARIA: Grease and dust.

ZERKOW: I could die and nobody ud know for days.
Grimy rags and rusty iron. Pull the knife out of my
heart.

MARIA: How?

(Pause)

ZERKOW: There was more than a hundred pieces?…

MARIA: …and all of `em gold…

(Dreaming again of the golden dishes, MARIA and ZERKOW exit the party.)

(18)

(Down the hall from the dental parlor. Later that night.)

(MISS BAKER and GRANNIS sit side by side, separated by an unseen wall.)

(He binds old magazines with a little device of his own invention, sewing the spines together with thread and a heavy needle.)

(She sips from a cup of tea.)

(In the hall outside, MCTEAGUE is saying goodnight to TRINA, as MARCUS sourly watches. The two old people— the doors to their rooms propped open—can listen in, and sometimes do. Now and then they glance at the wall between them.)

MCTEAGUE: Can you sleep?

TRINA: I don't know.

MCTEAGUE: Count sheep.

TRINA: Will that work? I'd get to four thousand nine hundred and ninety-nine—

MARCUS: *(A loud whisper)* Keep it down!

TRINA: Five thousand…

MARCUS: *(A loud whisper)* The geezers got their doors propped open again.

MCTEAGUE: You know what I think? We should buy five thousand lottery tickets.

TRINA: And what if not one of them won?

(McTEAGUE *works this out in his head.*)

McTEAGUE: We'd be back where we started, is all.

TRINA: *Alone.*

(McTEAGUE *realizes* TRINA'*s right. Offstage, a teakettle whistles.* GRANNIS *stops his work and looks at the wall.* MISS BAKER *exits into her kitchen.*)

McTEAGUE: Then what do *you* think we should do with the money?

TRINA: Invest it. Live on the income.

McTEAGUE: That wouldn't be much.

TRINA: But with that, and with what you make, and the money I get from my handicrafts...it oughta be plenty. We maybe could even start saving some.

McTEAGUE: I don't know—I just thought—five *thousand* dollars—buy us a *house*...

TRINA: Red velvet? Servants? A coach-in-four? Why not Buckingham Palace?

McTEAGUE: I'm silly, huh?

TRINA: You are. But I love you. Oh, Mac—do you love me?

(McTEAGUE *grabs* TRINA *and embraces her.* MISS BAKER *returns with her tea and sits down.* GRANNIS *resumes his binding.*)

MARCUS: Watchin' you recent magnets spoon is above and beyond the far call of my duty. We going to sleep with the dogs or not?

McTEAGUE: I'm coming.

(McTEAGUE *kisses* TRINA *and rushes off with* MARCUS. *She watches him go, then returns to the [offstage] dental parlors.*)

(GRANNIS and MISS BAKER are now alone. As he sews, GRANNIS jabs himself with his needle.)

GRANNIS: Bloody hell…

(Too late, GRANNIS remembers MISS BAKER. Guiltily, he looks at the wall. She frowns but tries to calm him, speaking softly:)

MISS BAKER: It's all right.

GRANNIS: It isn't. I never intended that you should see me, the way I was forced to present myself, tonight.

MISS BAKER: I thought you were very beautiful.

GRANNIS: Absent, I mean, cravat and collar. I think my shirt was even unbuttoned. Exposing to all the dry white hairs on my ancient chest. It was not in the guise of coot that I hoped we would finally meet.

MISS BAKER: We met already, remember, though? I dropped a day-old flounder at your feet.

GRANNIS: You did. And you turned so becoming a shade of pink that I thought I might…

MISS BAKER: What?

GRANNIS: Never mind.

(Pause)

MISS BAKER: If only…

GRANNIS: What?

MISS BAKER: Never mind. *(Pause)* If only I could tell you.

GRANNIS: If only I could tell *you.*

(In silence, GRANNIS sews and MISS BAKER drinks her tea.)

(19)

(GRANNIS's *veterinary clinic. Night.*)

(MCTEAGUE *and* MARCUS *enter the yard, where dogs are barking and whimpering.*)

MCTEAGUE: You think the ruckus'll keep us up?

MARCUS: Some of it I can stop with bones. That terrier's got gastritis, though. Not much we can do about that, for a fact. He's about to pass on, and it smarts. *(He speaks to the [offstage] dog.)* Hey, old son.

MCTEAGUE: I'm bushed, I guess. *(He starts to exit.)*

MARCUS: You owe me four bits.

(MCTEAGUE *stops, puzzled.*)

MCTEAGUE: I do?

MARCUS: That day I took you out to meet Trina. I paid for the ferry. Remember?

MCTEAGUE: That's so. You ought to have told me before. Here.

(MCTEAGUE *hands* MARCUS *the money.*)

MARCUS: It ain't a lot. But I need what I can get, nowadays.

MCTEAGUE: Are you broke?

MARCUS: And I'm sayin' nothing about you bedding down here.

MCTEAGUE: Should I pay for that too?

MARCUS: Well, your girl's asleep in your room. And her mother's in mine. Youda had to sleep somewheres, wouldn't you?

MCTEAGUE: All right, all right, I don't want you out on my account. Here's a dollar more…

(MARCUS *looks at the offered money.*)

MARCUS: Forget it.

McTEAGUE: No, take it.

MARCUS: FORGET IT.

(McTEAGUE *is puzzled by* MARCUS's *mood.*)

MARCUS: Let's call it a wedding present.

(*Pause*)

McTEAGUE: I want you to be the best man. Deal?

MARCUS: Go on an' get to bed.

(McTEAGUE *exits.* MARCUS *speaks to the dying dog.*)

MARCUS: Hey, old dog. You wanta know what? Yer troubles are just about over. Be up there in the clouds, with a buncha slow cats. Nice. Slow cats and bitches in heat forever. Fire hydrants like weeds, all over. Nicer than here. Maybe I oughta come with you, huh? Seein' as how I've tossed my life in the trash, like a sock fulla holes. Give up the girl—fine, all right…but *this*—throw five thousand dollars out a window—stuff it in somebody else's pockets? It mighta been mine. The girl *and* the money. And let it all blow away—for what? Because we were pals. Oh, "pals" is right—but five thousand—played it right into his hands—God *damn* the luck! "Best man"? (*Pause*) You want me to be the best man? (*Pause*) I don't think so, Mac. Forget a best man. I may be the worst man you'll ever hope to meet. (*He pulls a jackknife from his pocket, opens it up. He looks at the knife. Then he looks at the dying dog.*) You suffered too much, old son. You get a reward.

(*Knife in hands,* MARCUS *moves to the dog.*)

(20)

(*The dental parlor. The following day*)

(*A mysterious crate has appeared.*)

(McTEAGUE *comes in, pausing to say goodbye to* MARCUS.)

McTEAGUE: Thanks fer all yer help.

MARCUS: Forget it.

McTEAGUE: Giving yer room to Trina's mother and putting me up at the vet's an all—

MARCUS: My pleasure. I already give you my girl, am I right? An' I throw in a coupla thousand dollars, that comes with the girl I give to you. You want the shirt off my back? And that'll be it. (*He starts to tear off his shirt.*)

McTEAGUE: I don't want yer shirt—

MARCUS: I've thrown in everything else—

McTEAGUE: I don't want yer shirt!

MARCUS: But I guess you'll keep the five thousand. Huh?

McTEAGUE: It ain't mine to give back. Where the hell did you tie one on? It's not even noon.

MARCUS: I suppose, if I had as much money as you, I'd stay sober so I could enjoy it. (*He throws his shirt at the dentist's feet.*) My very last present to you. Pick it up.

McTEAGUE: I don't want it, I said.

MARCUS: PICK IT UP.

(*A standoff. Pause*)

MARCUS: Ain't you got any gratitude? Ain't you got any decency? You ten-cent zinc-pluggin' son-of-a-one-horse dentist!

(MARCUS *storms off.* McTEAGUE *is astonished.*)

McTEAGUE: "Zinc plugger?" (*He picks up* MARCUS's *shirt.*) I got no quarrel with you. (*Shaking his head, he goes into his room and finally sees the crate.*) What's this? (*He walks over to the crate and reads the label.*) "Dr McTeague, dentist—Polk Street, San Francisco, Cal. Via

Wells Fargo…" (*Excited, he tosses* MARCUS'*s shirt aside and pulls the lid off with just his bare hands.*)

(*The crate is packed with excelsior, on top of which is an envelope.*)

(MCTEAGUE *opens it and reads:*)

MCTEAGUE: "For my dear Mac's birthday, from Trina. The man will be round tomorrow to put it in place." (*He looks at the crate.*) Put *what* in place? (*Like a dog unearthing a bone, he digs away the excelsior, sending it flying all over. Then he gasps.*)

(MCTEAGUE *reaches into the crate and pulls out a huge tooth—a golden molar with giant prongs. It's so heavy he has to carefully put it down. As he stands aside to admire it,* MARCUS *enters.*)

MARCUS: I come back for my shirt. (*He sees the tooth.*) What in the hell is that?

MCTEAGUE: My tooth.

MARCUS: Where the hell did it come from?

MCTEAGUE: She gave it to me. For my birthday. Ain't she a jewel?

(MCTEAGUE, *entranced, stares at the tooth.*)

(MARCUS *stares at* MCTEAGUE.)

MARCUS: That tooth is mine.

(*As the lights fade out, the tooth glows brighter.*)

END OF ACT ONE

ACT TWO

(1)

(*Outside* McTeague's *new rooms, adjoining his dental parlor.*)

(*The giant golden tooth is hanging above the stage.*)

(The wedding and the wedding feast are over. The guests have left, except for Trina's Mother, who lingers to embrace her daughter, who's still in her wedding gown.

Trina's Father: (*Off*) Come, come, we miss the train.

Mother: I have to go.

(Trina's Mother *pulls away and stares at* Trina.)

Trina: Will Papa...?

Mother: The company tells him, "Pull the stakes, root your family up, move all the way to Los Angeles, why? Because there are *prospects*." Oh? "Less pay, a smaller house, longer day, but *prospects*." Ah. Papa believes them, though. Or he needs to believe. A man his age.

Trina: You?

Mother: I think we have prospects, sure. Two holes in the ground. Long and deep. I think we hold hands and jump in.

Trina: This is my *wedding* day!

MOTHER: And I talk like I talk. Because when will I see you again? Ever, when?

TRINA: Oh mamma, sometime…

(TRINA *holds her mother, who cries.*)

(*Inside the apartment,* MCTEAGUE *comes in, his shoes in hand, his morning coat removed and his shirt unbuttoned. Dazed by the massive banquet he's just polished off, he sits in his dental chair, drops his shoes and starts to nod.*)

(TRINA's MOTHER *pulls herself together.*)

MOTHER: My wedding night, I look at your father. Behind him a lamp on the mantel is lit. And the light is shining pink through his ears. And I never notice before, but now—his ears are made of gristle.

TRINA'S FATHER: (*Off*) Mamma!

MOTHER: Like a hog's. Gristle. I want to run.

TRINA: But you didn't.

MOTHER: No.

TRINA: Why didn't you?

MOTHER: Feel.

(*She takes* TRINA's *hand and puts it to her ear.*)

MOTHER: My ear is made of gristle, too.

TRINA'S FATHER: (*Off*) Mamma! The train!

MOTHER: It's time.

(MOTHER *gives* TRINA *a peck on the cheek and starts to hurry off.*)

(TRINA *runs after her, making her stop and embracing her.*)

TRINA: I'm afraid. Everything goes away. You go…

MOTHER: …and the fear will go away, too. Now run to your husband.

(TRINA's MOTHER disengages and exits. TRINA stares after her.)

TRINA: Mamma?

MOTHER: *(Off)* What is it, Trina?

(Pause)

TRINA: Nothing. Goodbye!

TRINA'S FATHER: *(Off)* Come, come, we miss the train.

TRINA: Mamma?

MOTHER: *(Farther off)* What is it?

TRINA: Goodbye.

MOTHER: *(Off)* Goodbye, little daughter.

(Far off, a door closes. MCTEAGUE, in his chair, wakes up.)

MCTEAGUE: Trina?

(TRINA freezes.)

MCTEAGUE: Are they gone?

TRINA: *(Quiet)* Yes.

(Not hearing TRINA, MCTEAGUE gets out of the chair and comes into the hall.)

MCTEAGUE: Gone?

(TRINA nods her head. MCTEAGUE crosses to her and puts a hand on her shoulder.)

TRINA: No! *(She flinches, drawing away.)*

MCTEAGUE: What's wrong?

(TRINA doesn't answer.)

MCTEAGUE: Trina? What is it?

TRINA: I can't...

MCTEAGUE: Can't what?

TRINA: I don't know. I'm afraid.

MᴄTᴇᴀɢᴜᴇ: Of what?

Tʀɪɴᴀ: I'm just afraid.

MᴄTᴇᴀɢᴜᴇ: You're here. With me. You're safe.

Tʀɪɴᴀ: I'm afraid of *you*.

(Pause)

MᴄTᴇᴀɢᴜᴇ: The time I knocked you out with ether…
the way you smell, and yer laugh in my ears, and yer
hair, and how kind you are, and yer skin…I wanted to
touch you. Lying there. Knocked out.

(Tʀɪɴᴀ trembles more.)

Tʀɪɴᴀ: Did you?

MᴄTᴇᴀɢᴜᴇ: I stopped myself.

Tʀɪɴᴀ: Why?

MᴄTᴇᴀɢᴜᴇ: Because I loved you.

(Pause)

*(As MᴄTᴇᴀɢᴜᴇ pulls Tʀɪɴᴀ to him, she gives herself up,
and they kiss a deep, passionate kiss.)*

(With her arms around his neck, she whispers:)

Tʀɪɴᴀ: You have to be good to me, Mac…

MᴄTᴇᴀɢᴜᴇ: I will.

Tʀɪɴᴀ: …you're all I have left in the world.

MᴄTᴇᴀɢᴜᴇ: It ain't other with me. But I *got* you, now. I
got you.

(MᴄTᴇᴀɢᴜᴇ and Tʀɪɴᴀ kiss again, overwhelmed.)

(2)

(MᴄTᴇᴀɢᴜᴇ and Tʀɪɴᴀ start to undress.)

*(In the hall outside their rooms, Zᴇʀᴋᴏᴡ hovers, trying to
overhear.)*

(MARIA *enters unseen, dressed in a raggedy robe, and watches* ZERKOW.)

(TRINA *steps out of her wedding dress; she's wearing corset and petticoats.* MCTEAGUE *takes off his coat and pants; he's wearing a fire-red union suit.*)

(TRINA *can't look at* MCTEAGUE; *he watches her.*)

MARIA: What do you hear?

(*Mortified,* ZERKOW *whirls around and stares at* MARIA.)

MARIA: Snoring? No?

ZERKOW: Don't you have you a narrow bed to crawl into?

MARIA: Narrow and *cold.* I'm in it. But then I hear steps. Like a thief in the night.

ZERKOW: I lost my wallet.

MARIA: Your wallet is in your pants. What are they doing?

(*Pause*)

ZERKOW: Nothing. Clothes are falling.

MARIA: *That's* something. What do you wish they was doing? Counting their money? (*She makes the sound of paper stacking:*) Whisht-whisht-whisht-whisht...

ZERKOW: It wouldn't be paper...

MARIA: Coins? (*He nods.*) Clink, clink, clink, clink...

(MCTEAGUE *pulls out of the top of his union suit, leaving the shirt-part dangling round his waist.*)

(*He approaches* TRINA, *who trembles.*)

MARIA: Gold?

(ZERKOW, *agonized, smiles.*)

MARIA: Twenty-dollar pieces?

ZERKOW: Why not?

MARIA: Sounds the same as dollar-pieces, you hear
it another way. Yes? "Clink, clink, clink, clink..."
Twenty, forty, sixty, eighty...or pick a stack up and
then let it fall out of your fingers, stack it again...*(Fast:)*
Clink-clink-clink-clink-clink...or you pile it up too
high...*(Slower:)* Clink...clink...clink...clink...

*(MCTEAGUE unties the laces of TRINA's corset. She holds
the garment up to her chest. He puts his arms around her
and kisses her hard on the mouth.)*

MARIA: Oh no, too tall, too tall, it's falling—click-
clackety-CLINK-CLANK-CLUNK...oh well...you got
time, you start over again...clink, clink, clink, clink...

*(Suddenly, MCTEAGUE sweeps TRINA up in his arms and
carries her off.)*

*(MARIA and ZERKOW are left alone on stage; Her mood
grows darker.)*

ZERKOW: And the golden plates?

MARIA: What about 'em?

ZERKOW: How did they sound?

MARIA: Like a crazy woman.

ZERKOW: No!

MARIA: They all say.

ZERKOW: They all of 'em live small lives the size of
beetles. *I* believe.

MARIA: Crazy greaser woman. Without a dime.

ZERKOW: But you had—your family had—a whole
chest of gold dishes—

MARIA: *Had.* Now I sell rags and bones to you. So I buy
a cheap polka dot scarf. Try to be one of the girls you
look at twice. But nobody looks even once.

ZERKOW: I'm looking.

MARIA: What do you see?

ZERKOW: Little girl in her very best party dress. In a great, dark room. At the end of a very long table all covered with snow-white lace. And the only light in the room is the table service...

MARIA: Golden plates...

ZERKOW: When you rapped 'em hard with a knuckle? How did they sound?

(Pause)

MARIA: Like church bells. No. Sweeter. Clearer.

ZERKOW: How...

MARIA: "Clang!"

ZERKOW: How?

MARIA: CLANG!

(MARIA *and* ZERKOW *are almost touching each other now.*)

ZERKOW: Again...

MARIA: *(Fading)* Clang...

ZERKOW: Don't let it die out.

MARIA: All lost.

ZERKOW: What's lost can always be found. Can't it?

(Pause)

MARIA: This great, dark room—I'm all alone?

ZERKOW: No. You look down the table, all the way to the other end. I raise a cup.

(ZERKOW *raises his hand and touches* MARIA's *face.*)

MARIA: I raise a cup too.

(MARIA *touches* ZERKOW's *face.*)

ZERKOW: A gold cup.

MARIA: All gold. Shining...

(3)

(MISS BAKER *is in the dentist's chair.*)

(TRINA, *in one of the waiting-chairs, whittles a little figurine, while* McTEAGUE *examines* MISS BAKER.)

TRINA: Is that a clean shirt?

McTEAGUE: It was clean last week.

TRINA: I'm washing your clothes more often, now. You don't have to wait that long.

MISS BAKER: I'm forgetting what I was dying to tell you. Maria Miranda Macapa? She's getting married.

McTEAGUE: To what?

MISS BAKER: To that rag-and-bone man Zerkow.

TRINA: No!

MISS BAKER: It's a fact. She asked me to make her a gown.

TRINA: What on earth do they see in each other?

McTEAGUE: Who else would have them?

MISS BAKER: He used to be a miner.

McTEAGUE: Was he?

MISS BAKER: The way I hear it, he and another prospector went out together. One of those horrible winters. Remember? And only Zerkow came down from the hills in the spring. They asked him why he was all alone. And you know what he said? "Meat is meat."

McTEAGUE: Open!

TRINA: "Meat is meat?"

McTEAGUE: Trina! Come help.

(TRINA *puts down her carving and crosses to* McTEAGUE, *who hands her a mallet.*)

TRINA: We haven't seen Mister Grannis lately.

MISS BAKER: *(Mouth open)* Eye-huh hah eye.

MCTEAGUE: Just rap that filling on in.

TRINA: You should tap on his door. See if he's well. Old people fall down...I don't mean *old*—

MISS BAKER: *(Mouth full)* Ee's oh-hay.

MCTEAGUE: *(Stepping back)* What?

MISS BAKER: He's O K. I hear him bustle about. Binding his magazines...

MCTEAGUE: Open!

TRINA: Tap harder?

MCTEAGUE: No. Just like you were doing.

(The LOTTERY AGENT comes in, sits down to wait.)

TRINA: How long have you worn your flannels?

MCTEAGUE: Why?

TRINA: I can smell you.

MCTEAGUE: So?

(TRINA hands MCTEAGUE the mallet and wanders away, upset.)

MCTEAGUE: I work, I sweat.

TRINA: ...and your feet are like hams and your socks are too thick, and so nothing will ever change. My *husband*. I'm bound to you for the rest of my life. Year after year, month after month, hour, minute, secondhand...same hands, same feet, same face, same breath, same husband, husband, husband...

MISS BAKER: I neh-huh mye-huh ha hell ha hah-nuh puh-pa-aye-shun.

MCTEAGUE: What?

MISS BAKER: I never minded the smell of honest...That night you won the lottery...when Mister Grannis came down in his shirtsleeves...

MCTEAGUE: *(Distracted by* TRINA*)* Did he?

MISS BAKER: He must have been out for a walk that day. I could smell the sea air on his skin, and I...

(In a reverie, MISS BAKER *gets out of the chair and exits the room, as the* LOTTERY AGENT *sits in the dentist's chair.)*

*(*MCTEAGUE *stares at* TRINA, *who's standing across the room, in tears.)*

MCTEAGUE: *(To* TRINA*)* Are you crying?

TRINA: Why can't you tell?

LOTTERY AGENT: It's official: six months from now— electrification of all of San Francisco. *(Pause)* I for one am not sure I can wait.

*(*MCTEAGUE *crosses to* TRINA. *He starts to unbutton his shirt.)*

MCTEAGUE: Are you crying?

TRINA: Not any more.

*(*MCTEAGUE *takes his shirt off; from a chair on which he's piled his clothes,* TRINA *hands him another he starts to put on.)*

MCTEAGUE: I'm changing my shirts twice a week.

TRINA: I know.

MCTEAGUE: And the collars and cuffs more often than that. And my flannels once a week.

TRINA: Oh, Mac...

MCTEAGUE: I can work on my patients and talk, all at once. I don't eat my peas with a knife any more. I've started to have opinions.

LOTTERY AGENT: *Three* months from now: incandescent light, at the flick of a switch.

MCTEAGUE: And I've started to dream.

TRINA: About what?

MCTEAGUE: A house of our own. Six rooms and a bath. Daylilies out front in the lawn. And a boy. Daniel…

TRINA: "Dan McTeague."

MCTEAGUE: An' *he* gets married. And *he* has children. And all of 'em settle with us in the house together. Nestled in. Like the way you fit all your animal carvings into that one little ark. And we get to be old, you an' me. An' yer hair turns white. And mine falls out. And it's like it was autumn. All the time. Sittin' right next to each other beside a window. Hear our kids and our grandkids, tearing around. And this autumn light coming in…

LOTTERY AGENT: Just a flick of a switch. Tomorrow…

(MARIA *comes in and begins to dust. She's hugely pregnant.*)

MARIA: You got any junk?

(*She's ignored.*)

(MCTEAGUE *puts on a stylish new coat.* TRINA *looks at the figure he cuts and starts to cry.*)

MCTEAGUE: What—what…?

TRINA: Old Mac, I love you so much. Are we happy together?

MCTEAGUE: Ain't we?

TRINA: I have to tell you something, though.

MCTEAGUE: Then tell me.

TRINA: It's terrible.

MCTEAGUE: What?

TRINA: I didn't love you. Before we were married.

McTEAGUE: You musta.

TRINA: I didn't! It's only now, after all these months…

McTEAGUE: You kissed me like you loved me. Down by the water, back then.

TRINA: I didn't. It's only now. Now I love you so much I'm afraid…

McTEAGUE: Afraid of what?

(TRINA *puts* McTEAGUE*'s hand to her ear.*)

TRINA: What's this?

McTEAGUE: *(Bewildered)* It's your ear.

TRINA: But what is it like?

McTEAGUE: It's like…an ear.

TRINA: It's gristle.

McTEAGUE: I guess it is.

TRINA: *(Anxious)* Is it?

McTEAGUE: I think you been working too hard.

TRINA: It's Christmas. Uncle needs all the toys I can make…

McTEAGUE: An' look at your fingers. Paint all over. You oughta wear gloves.

TRINA: Six months ago you'da kissed them anyway.

McTEAGUE: What?

TRINA: My dirty hands.

(*Embarrassed,* McTEAGUE *kisses* TRINA*'s hands.* MARIA *stops dusting to watch.*)

LOTTERY AGENT: Is that a picture?

MARIA: Won't last.

LOTTERY AGENT: You certain?

MARIA: What does?

(MARCUS, *unnoticed by* MCTEAGUE *and* TRINA, *comes in and sits down in a waiting-chair.*)

(MCTEAGUE *and* TRINA *embrace, as the others watch.*)

MARIA: *(To* MARCUS*)* Haven't seen you in a bit.

MARCUS: I been looking for ways to improve myself.

MARIA: No luck?

LOTTERY AGENT: If my watch is correct—and it is—one minute. And then…

MARIA: *(To* MARCUS*)* You didn't show up for the wedding.

MARCUS: Only so much of a crow a man can eat—

(MARIA *looks suddenly stricken; she hurries off.*)

MARCUS: Something I said?

MARIA: It's my time.

(MARIA *exits.* MARCUS *quietly speaks, to her back:*)

MARCUS: That's a baby? I thought you'd stuck a gold punch-bowl under your dress.

(TRINA *still clings to* MCTEAGUE, *unaware of the others in the room. He holds her, trying to comfort her—less passionate than consoling.*)

LOTTERY AGENT: Doctor McTeague?

(MARCUS *saunters up to the dental chair.*)

MARCUS: The good doctor's engaged some other wise. What is it?

LOTTERY AGENT: *(Referring to his watch)* It's almost time. For the City Electric.

MARCUS: Progress…

LOTTERY AGENT: Aren't you in favor?

MARCUS: I guess I've always had a soft spot for the dark.

LOTTERY AGENT: Then avert your gaze. 'Cause it's fleeting. Just about—*now.*

(Bright light comes flooding into the room. A muffled roar floats up from a crowd of people out on the street. MCTEAGUE and TRINA, embracing, don't notice.)

(The LOTTERY AGENT gets out of the chair and steps to the window, followed by MARCUS.)

LOTTERY AGENT: Is that a picture?

(Pause)

MARCUS: Look how far it lights up…

LOTTERY AGENT: This city is *big.*

MARCUS: All those people…back to empty rooms…

LOTTERY AGENT: At least they won't have to sit up in the dark.

MARCUS: You know about that?

LOTTERY AGENT: I work for the lottery company. Sure I know.

(MCTEAGUE and TRINA break their embrace. She hands him an elegant top hat, which he puts on.)

McTEAGUE: How do I look?

TRINA: Like a prince.

McTEAGUE: That makes you a princess, don't it?

TRINA: More like the girl in the cinders is how I look.

McTEAGUE: You got *me* duded up, you should treat yourself.

TRINA: We can't afford it.

McTEAGUE: Not even a single dress?

TRINA: Suppose you got sick?

McTEAGUE: Suppose the city fell down to the ground. Suppose we died. Can't we have fun before?

TRINA: What is fun?

(Pause)

McTEAGUE: You sittin' there in my lap, at the end of the day. Sharing a bottle of beer—not *steam*-beer, that's for the lower sorts—a bottle, watch that tooth you gave me catch the last light…

TRINA: You like your tooth?

McTEAGUE: I never liked anything more.

(McTEAGUE and TRINA embrace again. MARCUS turns from the window and watches.)

MARCUS: *(To the LOTTERY AGENT)* Drop all this money on people, and then—does it rankle? Watching 'em bask?

LOTTERY AGENT: Not that envy don't ever occur—but I try to remember: Everything goes away. Except love. Which is free. *(He tips his hat and exits.)*

MARCUS: Wanta bet? Ahem…

(McTEAGUE and TRINA break their embrace and turn, startled.)

TRINA: Marcus!

McTEAGUE: Where'd you come from?

MARCUS: Nice to see you likewise, cousin. Doctor…

TRINA: You didn't show up for the wedding, we thought…

MARCUS: I was looking for work.

TRINA: …and now all of this time has gone by…

McTEAGUE: We thought you was dead.

MARCUS: Not quite as much luck. I *am* moving.

TRINA: Where?

MARCUS: Down south. I'm off to be a cowboy.

McTEAGUE: You?

MARCUS: I met this English duck. Owns a ranch outside of Los Angeles. Untamed broncos…

McTEAGUE: What do you know about ranching?

MARCUS: I guess I can pick it up. You picked up teeth.

McTEAGUE: This yer idea of dreaming big?

TRINA: I think it sounds nice. Out under the stars, and the purple sage, and silver spurs…

MARCUS: Not as nice as a golden tooth, I know. But you take what you can get. So I'm leavin'. In just a few weeks. I thought we could have us a farewell picnic, like. You game?

(Pause)

TRINA: I don't know as we can afford it this month—

MARCUS: *(To* McTEAGUE*)* When she was a child, she useta pinch her pennies so hard they'd yelp. *(To* TRINA:*)* And now yer grown. Yer gettin' to be a miser. I thought you might.

McTEAGUE: She ain't either, it's just we live on a budget—

MARCUS: I'll pay. Up to the headlands, why don't we? Look out at the world together. One more time.

(4)

(The yard behind ZERKOW's *shack.)*

*(*MARIA, *no longer pregnant, hacks at the stage with a shovel.)*

*(*ZERKOW *enters and watches.)*

MARIA: The ground is too hard.

ZERKOW: Why are you digging?

MARIA: We got to put it someplace.

(Pause)

ZERKOW: They already took it away.

(MARIA stops.)

ZERKOW: What are you digging for?

(MARIA doesn't respond.)

ZERKOW: The gold?

MARIA: What gold?

ZERKOW: Your parents' plate.

MARIA: My what?

ZERKOW: Which you figured they must have lost, way back. 'Cause you knew it was gone. But what if it wasn't all lost so much as hidden?

MARIA: What was?

ZERKOW: If your parents had lived on this very spot? And they buried the gold in the yard. Or the walls? And maybe that's why you showed up at my door. You were only a child. But you still remembered. This place.

MARIA: The man I useta sell junk to died. That's why I showed up at your door.

ZERKOW: Still, it could be here.

MARIA: What could?

ZERKOW: "There was more than a hundred pieces" — remember? "And all of 'em gold…" You say it.

MARIA: Say what?

ZERKOW: "When you opened the lid, in the dark, it was like it was noon" …Remember?… "Dinner dishes and soup tureens, pitchers and platters and drinking mugs, a great big punch bowl carved with grapes—"

MARIA: MY BABY DIED.

(Pause)

ZERKOW: Better so. Another mouth.

MARIA: I remember my baby. I don't remember gold.

ZERKOW: They were both of 'em real. You held them up in your hands—

MARIA: I held my BABY.

ZERKOW: But long before that—you held a gold plate in your hand. And it rang like a bell.

MARIA: I don't know what you're talking about.

ZERKOW: "There was more than a hundred pieces." You *said*.

MARIA: Then I musta been crazy.

ZERKOW: *Now* you are.

MARIA: Now I see clear.

(MARIA *starts to exit.* ZERKOW *grabs her.*)

ZERKOW: Where is the gold?

MARIA: Where is my baby?

(Pause)

ZERKOW: In the ground.

MARIA: Then that's where you look. *(She exits.)*

ZERKOW: Where? *(Pause)* WHERE?

(5)

(TRINA's MOTHER *speaks a letter she's writing.*)

MOTHER: "My only girl: Your papa's business dims a little, day after day, and so, we look out. Again for `prospects'. Maybe New Zealand, he says, and I think, `You go to New Zealand alone'…Ach, Trina, I miss you so…"

(TRINA *enters, in a nicer dress, reading the letter aloud, watched by her* MOTHER.)

TRINA: "…I miss you so. If I know what else to do, I don't ask… But I don't know what to do. And I ask you before, but you don't reply, so I think the letter is lost."

MOTHER: Can you send your family fifty dollars?

TRINA: Fifty dollars?

McTEAGUE: (*Off*) Can't we?

TRINA: But fifty dollars is fifty dollars. That's two whole months of our interest.

McTEAGUE: (*Off*) Well, but you got a lot saved.

TRINA: Where?

McTEAGUE: (*Off*) In the chamois bag in the closet.

TRINA: A lot? I don't think I've got thirty.

McTEAGUE: (*Off*) Come on! I guess you got nearer a *hundred* and thirty.

TRINA: I don't!

(McTEAGUE *enters.*)

McTEAGUE: You want somebody to find your family dead at the kitchen table? Right next to the rat?

TRINA: I never asked *them* for money.

McTEAGUE: When did you have to?

(*Pause*)

TRINA: We can give them twenty-five. And that's all. You send half and so will I. Twelve and a half apiece. Will that do?

McTEAGUE: I guess it'll have to, won't it?

(MCTEAGUE *pulls out some money, and hands it to* TRINA's MOTHER.)

(TRINA's MOTHER *waits for* TRINA's *half, but* TRINA *turns away.*)

TRINA: We should run. We're late for Cousin Mark's picnic.

(MCTEAGUE *and* TRINA *exit, leaving* TRINA's MOTHER, *who watches them go.*)

(6)

(*The headlands.* TRINA *enters, followed by* GRANNIS, *who's lugging a heavy picnic basket.*)

TRINA: I can carry awhile—

GRANNIS: I'm only ancient, Mrs McTeague. Not decrepit.

TRINA: (*Looking around*) Here?

GRANNIS: I think so. Yes. (*He puts the basket down and looks out.*) The ocean beyond, and the bay behind…

TRINA: Put you in mind of the English coast?

GRANNIS: A little. Wilder, though. I feel much smaller, here.

TRINA: Miss Baker says you're the youngest son of a baronet. Cruelly wronged.

GRANNIS: Miss Baker's remarkably silly. For one of her age. Our age.

TRINA: Do you love her?

GRANNIS: I beg your pardon?

TRINA: Do you?

(*Pause*)

GRANNIS: I should have thought it was obvious.

TRINA: Why haven't you married her, then?

GRANNIS: We've only spoken once in ten years. She dropped a fish. I picked it up. It seemed an inopportune moment to ask for her hand.

TRINA: *(Shielding her eyes)* Where is she?

GRANNIS: She's down below, in the meadow, watching the games. She said the heights were making her dizzy.

TRINA: It wasn't the heights.

(Pause)

GRANNIS: Why are they chucking that boulder about?

TRINA: To see who can throw it the farthest.

(A rock comes thumping onto the stage.)

GRANNIS: Your husband.

(TRINA looks off at the struggling men.)

TRINA: He's very strong. He butted a man through a door, one time—

GRANNIS: —with his head. So he told me twice, today. You look at him so oddly.

TRINA: I do?

GRANNIS: ...as he vies for your attention.

TRINA: Mine? I think it's other men a man wants to impress. *(To change the subject, she begins to unpack the basket. She pulls a tablecloth out and spreads it.)*

GRANNIS: Do you hope to have children?

TRINA: Someday...

GRANNIS: How long will you wait?

TRINA: How long will you wait for Miss Baker? *(Pause)* Do we seem to be young? My husband and me?

GRANNIS: Younger than I've any hope of being.

TRINA: But young enough to change? We aren't. Which makes us as old as you.

GRANNIS: Do you need to change?

TRINA: I'm growing stingier. Day by day. It's just the way I am. I can't help it. And Mac'll keep pulling out teeth with his hands. Which is all he's ever known how to do. And the nicer people will go to the fancier dentist down the block. Forever and ever and ever.

(Pause)

GRANNIS: Do you love him?

TRINA: *(Evading, as she points to the horizon)* I'd like to go off in one of those ships. Just away and away and away…

GRANNIS: Where?

TRINA: Any where.

GRANNIS: Away from Doctor McTeague?

TRINA: No. With him. Away from—this.

GRANNIS: "This"?

TRINA: All this. The grocer's bills and the nagging parents, mooching friends and floors to clean, the leaking roof and the lingering cough, and the never being certain—

GRANNIS: Of what?

(Pause)

TRINA: Never being certain. *(Pause)* I think you should marry Miss Baker tomorrow. Sail away.

GRANNIS: We don't have any money.

TRINA: Money's for all the uncertainty. You'd be sailing away from that.

(MISS BAKER hurries in, upset. TRINA whispers:)

TRINA: Ask her now—

MISS BAKER: Somebody do something!

GRANNIS: What is it?

MISS BAKER: They started to wrestle, and Doctor McTeague had pinned him easy, and walked away, but then Marcus jumped him, and—oh!

(MARCUS and MCTEAGUE tumble on stage together, rolling around like fighting dogs.)

MISS BAKER: DO something!

MCTEAGUE: He bit my EAR!

MARCUS: God damn you, get OFF of me!

(MCTEAGUE, on top, is pushing MARCUS' face in the dirt.)

TRINA: Mac! Let him go!

MCTEAGUE: *(To MARCUS)* You wanta eat something? Do ya? Huh?

MISS BAKER: Mister Grannis, stop it! Make them stop!

(Fearful, GRANNIS hesitates.)

GRANNIS: That's enough now, Doctor McTeague—

MARCUS: Yer chokin'—

MCTEAGUE: I wanta be!

MISS BAKER: *(To GRANNIS)* How can you stand there?

GRANNIS: Doctor McTeague?…

(Frantic, TRINA wades in and slaps MCTEAGUE, hard.)

(Suddenly, MCTEAGUE slams his opponent against the ground a final time, leaps up and grabs TRINA.)

MCTEAGUE: You hit me.

TRINA: You didn't know what you were doing.

(MARCUS, half on hands and knees, is scrambling off the stage.)

MCTEAGUE: He almost bit my ear clean off.

TRINA: He's an animal, then. Let him go.

(Frightened and furious, MARCUS exits.)

McTEAGUE: You hit me.

TRINA: Then you hit me. If it has to be that. An eye for an eye.

(MCTEAGUE sinks to his knees, desolate.)

GRANNIS: Can I offer a laundered handkerchief, Doctor McTeague?

MISS BAKER: Oh, that's good. That you step in now.

(GRANNIS forces himself to look at MISS BAKER.)

GRANNIS: I was afraid.

MISS BAKER: I saw. *(Upset, she turns and hurries off.)*

TRINA: Could *I* have it?

(TRINA takes the handkerchief from the dashed old man.)

TRINA: Thank you, Mister Grannis—

GRANNIS: For nothing whatever. At least I can help you back down—

TRINA: We can manage.

GRANNIS: Then… *(Abashed, he exits.)*

(TRINA dabs at the blood on MCTEAGUE's head with the handkerchief. (He keeps wincing and pulling away, but she continues.)

TRINA: Why were you fighting?

McTEAGUE: We wasn't fighting, at first. It was just a game. But I won. And he says I always won. And he jumped on my back.

TRINA: What did he mean—you always win.

McTEAGUE: He meant you.

(Pause)

TRINA: Do you love me?

McTEAGUE: What are you talking about?

TRINA: As much as when we was married?

McTEAGUE: You know I do.

TRINA: But I want you to say. Of your own accord.

McTEAGUE: I don't understand.

TRINA: Say "I love you".

(Pause)

McTEAGUE: I love you. *(Pause)* That better?

(TRINA warily strokes his bloody head, as if petting a savage dog.)

TRINA: Look at that ship out there.

McTEAGUE: What about it?

(TRINA doesn't answer. They both stare out.)

(7)

(GRANNIS and MISS BAKER sit side by side again, between them the unseen wall. She holds a forgotten cup of tea in her lap; he, some magazines he isn't binding. She looks at the wall, then away. He does the same.)

GRANNIS: *(Remembering)* "Oh, that's good. That you step in *now*."

(Distraught, GRANNIS gets to his feet with such force he knocks over his chair, scattering magazines. MISS BAKER starts and looks at the wall. Embarrassed, GRANNIS rights his chair and starts to pick up the magazines.)

(In the hall outside, MARIA appears, disheveled and frantic.)

MARIA: Mister Grannis, oh, please, let me in!

GRANNIS: It's open...

(MARIA *runs in.* MISS BAKER *attends the following with the greatest attention, pressing her ear to the unseen wall.*)

MARIA: He's after me. With a knife.

GRANNIS: Who is?

MARIA: With a knife this long. It's Zerkow. Listen: It's *him.*

ZERKOW: *(Off)* Maria!

MARIA: I knock at the doors below, but nobody opens. Don't let him get me, will you?

GRANNIS: No...

(ZERKOW *appears in the hall, enraged.*)

ZERKOW: I know where you are. In that codger's room—

GRANNIS: I beg your pardon—

ZERKOW: —you ought to be ashamed!

GRANNIS: How long was that knife?

(MARIA *holds her hands far apart—very long.*)

GRANNIS: Mister Zerkow?

ZERKOW: Tell my wife to come out right now, you lecherous buzzard.

GRANNIS: She says you've got a knife.

ZERKOW: Wanta see it?

GRANNIS: I've got a revolver.

MARIA: *(Whispered)* Do you?

(GRANNIS *shakes his head.*)

GRANNIS: I want to hear your footsteps clomping rapidly down the stairs.

ZERKOW: Or what?

GRANNIS: Or I'm firing through the door. You son-of-a-bitch!

ZERKOW: I want my wife!

GRANNIS: Go home!

(Pause)

ZERKOW: I'll do for you yet, my girl. Come see if I won't.

(ZERKOW exits. MISS BAKER steps fearfully into the hall and looks around. She moves to GRANNIS' door, wanting to knock.)

GRANNIS: Now what was that all about?

MARIA: I woke up about an hour ago, I had a bad dream, he wasn't in bed. I wanted somebody to hold me. So I look around and I see him, down on his knees by a hole in the floor. He's ripped the floor-boards up, and he's digging inside with a knife, and he's mumbling: "More'n a hundred pieces, and all of 'em gold. More'n a hundred pieces, all of 'em gold." Then I guess he feels me looking at him. He comes over to me, and the moonlight's shining the knife, and he says, "Where is it?" I say, "Where's what?" He says, "I know you hid it someplace, so tell me where. Or I'll cut you."

GRANNIS: Why did you ever make up that story?

MARIA: What story?

GRANNIS: About the gold dishes.

MARIA: I never heard of any gold dishes. What are you talking about?

(MISS BAKER knocks.)

MISS BAKER: Mister Grannis? Is everything all right?

GRANNIS: *(Ignoring)* Would you like the key to my clinic? I've got a cot—

MARIA: I'll see if he's sleeping, first. I can hide the knife. Then I won't be afraid.

MISS BAKER: Mr Grannis?

GRANNIS: You won't reconsider?

MARIA: I land on my feet.

GRANNIS: Then good night, Maria. And tell the old woman next door to mind her business.

MARIA: Thank you, Mister Grannis. Good night.

(MARIA *steps into the hall, confronting* MISS BAKER.)

MISS BAKER: What's happening?

MARIA: Nothing you need to know, he says. Go drink some tea.

(MARIA *exits, leaving* MISS BAKER *alone in the hall, bereft, as* GRANNIS *stares at the door, unable to move.*)

(8)

(*The dental parlor. Early evening.*)

(MCTEAGUE, *in his fanciest clothes and top hat, sits in his chair, waiting for* TRINA.)

MCTEAGUE: You plannin' still on a promenade?

TRINA: (*Off*) I've got so much paint on my hands—

MCTEAGUE: Wear gloves!

(TRINA *enters, nicely dressed and pulling on gloves.*)

TRINA: That new department store on Kearny—

MCTEAGUE: —one with the big rotunda?

TRINA: Miss Baker told me they have a band.

MCTEAGUE: You wanta go there?

(TRINA *stares at* MCTEAGUE.)

MCTEAGUE: Trina? What's wrong?

TRINA: Nothing. I just—I was looking at you, and you looked so nice, and I…wanted to touch you.

McTEAGUE: Well, that's all right…

TRINA: Do you want to touch me?

(Pause)

McTEAGUE: Sure, I guess—

TRINA: You don't. Do you?

McTEAGUE: *(Bewildered)* I thought we was going downtown.

TRINA: *(Rebuffed)* Then let's.

McTEAGUE: Come here.

TRINA: What?

McTEAGUE: Come here!

(TRINA crosses to the chair and McTEAGUE pulls her into his lap.)

TRINA: We're going to miss the band.

McTEAGUE: The band can hang. Look out at the night.

(Holding each other close, McTEAGUE and TRINA look out the window.)

TRINA: What's that glimmer, far off?

McTEAGUE: It's the public baths on Grant, I think. They got a glass roof and it catches the moon… Hear that honking?

TRINA: What is it?

McTEAGUE: Geese at the market across the street.

TRINA: Listen: way far off…

McTEAGUE: That's the Sacramento train…

(A POSTMAN with a bag of mail approaches, stepping out of the shadows.)

POSTMAN: Doctor McTeague?

(Embarrassed and startled, TRINA *clambers out of her husband's lap.)*

McTEAGUE: What the hell do you want?

POSTMAN: I knocked, but you musta not heard. And the door was open. Special Delivery.

*(*POSTMAN *hands* McTEAGUE *a letter.)*

McTEAGUE: From City Hall?

POSTMAN: Sign?

(The POSTMAN *offers a form and a pen;* McTEAGUE *scratches his signature.)*

POSTMAN: Thank you. You want I should close the door behind me?

TRINA: Please.

POSTMAN: Enjoy the night.

(The POSTMAN *exits as* McTEAGUE *tears open the envelope and inspects the letter.)*

TRINA: City Hall?

McTEAGUE: I guess.

TRINA: What could they want with us?

McTEAGUE: I don't know. I can't figure it out. You read it.

*(*TRINA *looks at the letter.)*

TRINA: "...whereas the aforesaid Mr McTeague"— don't they mean *Doctor* McTeague?—"has never received a diploma from an accredited college of dentistry, the aforesaid Mr McTeague is enjoined from the further practice of his profession..." *(She drops the letter.)* Oh, Mac...

McTEAGUE: What does it mean? "Enjoined?

TRINA: Prohibited. Prevented.

McTEAGUE: From what?

TRINA: From doing your job.

McTEAGUE: Why?

(Pause)

TRINA: How did you learn to be a dentist?

McTEAGUE: I went along with a fellow who came to the mine. My mother sent me. We used to go from one camp to another. I sharpened his excavators for him and put his notices up. He had a wagon.

(Pause)

TRINA: But didn't you never go to a college?

McTEAGUE: No, I never went. *(Pause)* I was a car-boy. Down in the mines. And then I went off with the fellow.

(Pause)

TRINA: Then you haven't the right to call yourself a doctor.

McTEAGUE: What do you mean? I've been practicing here ten years.

TRINA: But it's the law. You can't practice, or call yourself a doctor, unless you've got a diploma.

McTEAGUE: What's that?

TRINA: It's a kind of paper you get—. It don't matter. We're ruined.

McTEAGUE: But ain't I a dentist? Look at that golden tooth out there. I've been practicing all my life. They can't ask me to stop.

TRINA: They ain't askin' you, Mac. You're *enjoined*.

McTEAGUE: How are they going to know if I practice or not?

TRINA: How do they know you never went to school?

(*Pause*)

McTEAGUE: But ain't I a dentist anyway? I've been practicing all my life.

TRINA: If you had to stop—

McTEAGUE: I ain't quitting for just a piece of paper.

TRINA: —we couldn't afford these rooms.

McTEAGUE: We got your money—

TRINA: —the *interest*, Mac. We can't touch the money.

McTEAGUE: We couldn't get by on the interest only. Could we?

(*Pause*)

TRINA: Maybe nobody will know.

(*Pause*)

McTEAGUE: I ain't quitting for just a piece of paper.

TRINA: No, don't.

McTEAGUE: I got a full slate tomorrow.

TRINA: Keep it. Maybe nobody will know.

(*Pause*)

McTEAGUE: Do you want to go out?

TRINA: It's late.

(McTEAGUE *removes his top hat, squashes it down.*)

(9)

(*The dental parlor. Day*)

(McTEAGUE *is finishing up with* MARIA, *who has a shiner.* TRINA, *looking gloomy, assists.*)

(MISS BAKER *nervously sits in a waiting-chair.*)

MARIA: You close a bar down?

MCTEAGUE: I didn't. Why?

MARIA: You shake so much, you hurt me today.

MCTEAGUE: I'm sorry.

MARIA: Don't mention it—yowdj!

(MCTEAGUE *pulls back to steady himself.* TRINA *tries to make conversation.*)

TRINA: How did you get a black eye?

MARIA: I run into a door. Over and over and over…

TRINA: Your husband?

MARIA: "Nothing works out," he says. He drinks…

TRINA: You could knock some sense into him…

MARIA: Makes it worse. You hump your back, and it's soonest over. *(To* MCTEAGUE:*)* We done?

MCTEAGUE: For today. Let your nerves unjangle.

MARIA: It ain't *my* nerves.

(MARIA *gets out of the chair and exits.* MISS BAKER *remains in her seat, apprehensive.*)

TRINA: You ought to change out of that coat.

MCTEAGUE: Why?

TRINA: If you dirty it now, we can't pay to clean it.

MCTEAGUE: Ain't I working, still?

TRINA: For how long?

(Pause)

MCTEAGUE: Who did this to us?

TRINA: I don't know.

(MCTEAGUE *removes his elegant coat and puts on an older, shabbier one.*)

MCTEAGUE: Miss Baker?

(MISS BAKER *nervously settles herself in the dental chair.*)

MCTEAGUE: How are you?

MISS BAKER: I'm old. How are you?

TRINA: Getting older likewise. How's Mister Grannis?

MISS BAKER: He's dead.

(MCTEAGUE *and* TRINA *are astonished.*)

TRINA: What?

MISS BAKER: To me, at least. I all but called him a coward.

TRINA: *(Recovering from her shock)* Is he?

MISS BAKER: Probably not.

TRINA: Apologize.

MISS BAKER: That would be hard.

TRINA: Because…

MISS BAKER: I'm a coward.

(*At this moment the* POSTMAN *suddenly reappears.*)

POSTMAN: Doctor McTeague?

(MCTEAGUE *and* TRINA *stare at each other.*)

MCTEAGUE: From City Hall?

(*The* POSTMAN *hands the letter over.*)

POSTMAN: You're popular. Sign?

(MCTEAGUE *signs and the* POSTMAN *exits.*)

MISS BAKER: Special Delivery?

(MCTEAGUE *tears open the letter.* TRINA, *in agony, watches him read.*)

TRINA: What?

MCTEAGUE: It says, "Cease and desist immediately… under penalty of prosecution…"

MISS BAKER: Cease and desist from what?

MCTEAGUE: You have to go home.

MISS BAKER: But the toothache's back—

MCTEAGUE: There's a fancier dentist. Down the road.

MISS BAKER: Aren't you well?

MCTEAGUE: No. I—no.

(MISS BAKER gets out of the chair.)

MISS BAKER: Can I make another appointment?

MCTEAGUE: Next week—

TRINA: —is not good. My husband has to rest.

MISS BAKER: Then I hope he's better soon.

TRINA: Thank you, Miss Baker. Goodbye.

(MISS BAKER exits.)

MCTEAGUE: Who did this to us?

(It occurs to both of them, suddenly.)

MCTEAGUE & TRINA: Marcus…

(Pause)

MCTEAGUE: I'll kill him.

TRINA: How? He's moved. *(Pause)* We have to move too.

(They all look at each other. The lights fade.)

END OF ACT TWO

ACT THREE

(1)

(A new room—much smaller and dirtier.)

(The giant golden tooth is on the floor, to one side. Beside it rests the canary cage, and McTeague's *slate appointment board.)*

*(*McTeague *and* Trina *are changing into dingier clothes.)*

McTeague: I can't live in this place.

Trina: Then don't.

(Pause)

McTeague: It's like a cage. I keep barking my shins on the tooth—

Trina: Sell it.

McTeague: You gave it to me. *(Pause)* You gave it to me.

(Pause)

Trina: You have to find a new job.

McTeague: I will.

Trina: Doing what?

(Pause)

McTeague: Five thousand dollars…

Trina: Is all that can save us.

McTEAGUE: Then let it save us now. We can live on the money until—

TRINA: Until when? There ain't an "until" in the picture, Mac. What do you think will change? Tell me. Find a new job—doing *what*?

(Pause)

McTEAGUE: It smells like somebody's hair-oil…

TRINA: Does it?

McTEAGUE: …that died a bad death in this room.

TRINA: Get used to it, then.

McTEAGUE: I won't. How much have you got in that chamois bag?

TRINA: That money is all I've saved. And it's less than eighty—

McTEAGUE: Two hundred you mean.

TRINA: Not even eighty.

McTEAGUE: But can't we use some of *that* money, at least—to fix up?

TRINA: That money is just for emergencies.

McTEAGUE: What is *this*, then?

(Pause)

TRINA: This is a room that ought to be good enough.

McTEAGUE: It's small and it's dirty and smells.

TRINA: Then live in a palace, why don'tcha? And *you* pay the rent.

(Pause)

McTEAGUE: I never thought of my doctor's fees as *mine*, when I was working. We lumped everything together.

TRINA: Exactly. And I'm the one that's working now. I'm making toys, and you're not lumping in anything.

(Pause)

McTEAGUE: I'm going to get a bottle of beer.

TRINA: We can't afford it. It's fifteen cents.

McTEAGUE: But I haven't had a swallow of beer in three weeks.

TRINA: Drink steam-beer, then. You've got a nickel.

McTEAGUE: I don't like steam-beer now.

TRINA: Get used to it. *(Pause)* You were used to it, once.

McTEAGUE: I was somebody other, then.

(There's a knock at the door.)

TRINA: Come in?

(The FANCY DENTIST *waltzes in.)*

FANCY DENTIST: Allow me to introduce myself—

McTEAGUE: No need. Yer that fancy dentist down the block.

(The FANCY DENTIST *bows.)*

FANCY DENTIST: They tell me, Doctor, you're leaving our fair profession.

McTEAGUE: Retiring, yes.

FANCY DENTIST: Then I don't suppose you've got any further use for that golden tooth.

McTEAGUE: I guess not.

FANCY DENTIST: What do you say to ten dollars?

McTEAGUE: Ten dollars?

FANCY DENTIST: Well what do *you* reckon it's worth?

McTEAGUE: A lot more—

TRINA: But ten dollars—

McTEAGUE: —it was a *gift.*

(MCTEAGUE's *look shames* TRINA.)

FANCY DENTIST: I understand. I also could use an appointment-slate—

TRINA: We have one of those—

McTEAGUE: —but it ain't for sale.

TRINA: —for less than two bits.

FANCY DENTIST: Two bits it is.

(*Ignoring* MCTEAGUE, *the* FANCY DENTIST *gives* TRINA *a quarter.*)

(*She gives him a slate covered with chalked-in names.*)

McTEAGUE: The chalk is extra.

FANCY DENTIST: (*Of the names on the slate*) These the last people you saw?

McTEAGUE: Get out.

FANCY DENTIST: You mind if I rub 'em off?

McTEAGUE: Get OUT.

FANCY DENTIST: You don't want to trade anything for a diploma, do you?

(FANCY DENTIST *exits with the slateboard, winking.* MCTEAGUE *and* TRINA *look at each other.*)

TRINA: How did he know?

McTEAGUE: Everyone must know. (*Pause*) Get used to it.

TRINA: Are you crying?

(*Pause*)

McTEAGUE: It's just—I wake up early, still, and I think, "Now who am I seein' this afternoon? There's Vanovitch at two o'clock, and Heise's little girl at three… Who else is coming?" And then I remember: nobody's coming. Ever again.

TRINA: Oh, Mac…

McTEAGUE: And our flat is gone, and our furniture…

(TRINA *picks up a piece of chalk, left behind from the slate board, and starts to draw large outlines on the floor.*)

TRINA: We have to not panic…

McTEAGUE: What are you doing?

TRINA: We have to remember the way it all was.

McTEAGUE: Better off letting it fade.

TRINA: No, I WON'T…the melodeon, see, was in front of the window, here, where I'm drawing a box…and the parlor table was here, a circle…and here would have been the mantelpiece, with your little stone dog, and the vase of poppies my cousin painted on velvet, above it…

McTEAGUE: And where are my patients?

(TRINA*'s brought up short; she looks around.*)

TRINA: And where's your chair?… (*She stares at the floor.*) You have to let me hope.

McTEAGUE: But hope for less. (*He kneels beside her, stroking her hair.*)

(TRINA *starts to rub out a chalk outline with her hand.*)

TRINA: Help me.

(McTEAGUE, *on hands and knees, begins to rub one of the outlines off.*)

TRINA: With the money we save on rent…

McTEAGUE: What?

TRINA: We could buy your instruments back.

McTEAGUE: And then what?

(Pause. TRINA *remembers, suddenly.)*

TRINA: I forgot. I keep forgetting.

McTEAGUE: Nobody's coming. Ever again.

*(*McTEAGUE *and* TRINA *continue rubbing the outlines out.)*

(2)

*(*ZERKOW'*s hovel.* MARIA *is kneeling beside a hole, where he has ripped the floorboards up.* MISS BAKER *timidly enters.)*

MISS BAKER: Maria?

MARIA: *(Not looking up)* Name's Maria Miranda Macapa... Had a flying squirrel an' let him go.

MISS BAKER: Mister Grannis pawned a little device—for binding up old magazines. I thought I might buy it back.

MARIA: You see it?

*(*MISS BAKER *looks around, nervous.)*

MISS BAKER: No, but you couldn't have sold it. It isn't of any value...

MARIA: Maybe it's down in this hole. With the rest of the treasure.

MISS BAKER: What treasure?

MARIA: My husband says there is gold in the walls.

MISS BAKER: He used to be a miner?

MARIA: Up in the hills.

MISS BAKER: He spent too much time alone.

MARIA: So did I. So did you. I don't see no magazine-gadget. Sorry. *(She points off:)* Take your geezer a rusty bicycle wheel.

*(*MISS BAKER *kneels beside the hole.)*

MISS BAKER: *Is* there anything down there?

MARIA: *(Shrugging)* My husband gets so stinking drunk, he rips it up and then he forgets to look.

(Instinctively, MISS BAKER *sticks her arm in the hole.)*

MARIA: I think about looking. And then I think about snakes.

(With a jerk, MISS BAKER *pulls out of the hole.)*

MISS BAKER: I felt something.

MARIA: Scaly?

MISS BAKER: No. Like cloth.

*(*MARIA *reaches far into the hole. She withdraws her arm; her hand is clutching a large dirty sack like a laundry bag, its mouth knotted shut.)*

MISS BAKER: Well, what is it?

MARIA: It's heavy…

MISS BAKER: Open it!

MARIA: No.

MISS BAKER: Why not?

MARIA: I'm afraid.

MISS BAKER: But what if your husband was right? What if it's all the golden plate?

MARIA: But what if it's not? *(Pause)* He beats me. And then after he beats me, he wants me. But he can't have me. *(Pause)* He has me, but I'm gone.

MISS BAKER: If this is the golden service, Maria, you could be gone for real.

*(*MARIA *considers. Then she starts to unknot the sack.)*

(She looks inside.)

MARIA: Oh…

MISS BAKER: Is it…

(MARIA *reaches into the bag.*)

MARIA: More than a hundred pieces, and all of 'em… *(She pulls a rusty can out.)* …tin. Tin plates, tin knives and forks, tin pots and pans… A bag of junk 'got shoved out of sight…

(She empties the bag of junk on the stage. Then she starts laughing.)

MISS BAKER: Don't…

(MARIA *begins to gather the junk and stuff it back in the bag.*)

MARIA: I can hide it again. Let him find it. Let him hope.

MISS BAKER: Won't that hurt him?

MARIA: Won't it? Oh—like a knife.

MISS BAKER: Then won't he hurt you?

(MARIA *keeps stuffing the bag with junk.*)

MISS BAKER: I don't think you should do this. Maria? Maria—

MARIA: Name's Maria Miranda Macapa. Had a flying squirrel an' let him go. What did you say you was after, again?

MISS BAKER: A device for binding magazines. It belonged to Mr Grannis, you see, and it helped him pass the time.

MARIA: How much has he got to pass? *(She knots the mouth of the bag.)*

(Unnoticed, ZERKOW *enters and watches the ladies.)*

MARIA: Don't love him.

MISS BAKER: No?

MARIA: It won't be long: into a hole in the ground… *(She stuffs the bag into the hole in the floor.)* …like this.

(ZERKOW's eyes are glittering, as he watches.)

MARIA: Dust to dust...

(3)

(The McTEAGUES' new room.)

(TRINA sits in a chair, painting a toy. She's wearing a shabby housecoat. Her once-beautiful hair is unkempt.)

(McTEAGUE comes in; he's wet. He stares at TRINA.)

TRINA: Did you find a job?

McTEAGUE: You notice sumthin'?

(TRINA looks up.)

TRINA: You're drunk.

McTEAGUE: That ain't it.

TRINA: You are drunk.

McTEAGUE: I'm wet. You wouldn'ta noticed. I'm soppin'.

TRINA: It's raining?

McTEAGUE: Didn't I *say* it was gonna pour? Didn't I ask for a nickel to ride the trolley? I walked in the rain for an hour. You didn't look up.

TRINA: I'm working.

McTEAGUE: Well, stop.

(TRINA continues.)

McTEAGUE: I said stop.

TRINA: *Did* you find a job?

(McTEAGUE crosses to her and knocks the carving and brush from her hand.)

McTEAGUE: I said stop.

(Pause)

TRINA: What do you want me to do?

McTEAGUE: Just sit there. Watch the night come on.

(Pause)

TRINA: Nobody was hiring?

McTEAGUE: No.

(Pause)

TRINA: You told me you never drank anything stronger than beer.

McTEAGUE: You told me you loved me.

(Pause)

TRINA: I do love you.

McTEAGUE: Then give me a dollar.

TRINA: Why?

McTEAGUE: For a piece of meat. You got three hundred dollars—

TRINA: I don't.

McTEAGUE: —in that bag you got hidden under your robe. You think I don't know what you do? I put my eye to the keyhole, Trina. I watch you count your money. Over and over. I watch you polish it, piece by piece. I seen you put some of the change in your mouth. Jingle it in your cheeks. I want you to spit some out.

TRINA: No.

(McTEAGUE grabs TRINA's hand.)

McTEAGUE: Stuff your cheeks with coins, I couldn't believe my eyes. Like this.

(McTEAGUE crams TRINA's fingers into his mouth and bites down.)

TRINA: You're hurting me.

(MCTEAGUE *grunts.*)

TRINA: Mac, stop!

(MCTEAGUE *bites harder.*)

TRINA: What do you WANT!

(MCTEAGUE *pulls* TRINA'*s fingers out of his mouth.*)

MCTEAGUE: I said. A dollar.

(TRINA *pulls the chamois bag from under her chair.*)

TRINA: Do you know how much you just hurt me?

MCTEAGUE: No. Tell me. *(Pause)* TELL me.

(TRINA *pulls a coin out of the bag and gives it to*
MCTEAGUE.)

TRINA: You broke the skin.

MCTEAGUE: Good. *(Of the coin)* This ain't enough.

(TRINA *hesitates.* MCTEAGUE *grabs her hand and again
bites down on her fingers. She screams.*)

MCTEAGUE: You want more? Give me another dollar.

(*With trembling fingers,* TRINA *pulls out another coin and
holds it out to* MCTEAGUE. *He grabs it and turns to walk
away.*)

TRINA: Where are you going?

MCTEAGUE: Fishing.

TRINA: You said it was raining.

MCTEAGUE: The fish'll bite all the better for that.

TRINA: You could bring a fish home…

MCTEAGUE: Might save you a nickel, mightn't it?

TRINA: And if it did? *(Pause)* You could let me come…

MCTEAGUE: I like to be alone when I fish. I make me a
fire, and grill my catch on a stick, and eat it slow. The
whole thing, right down to the head.

(Pause)

TRINA: Does it make you happy?

McTEAGUE: I useta eat fish like that when I was a kid. Up in the mountains. Before I started to work in the mine.

TRINA: How can you build a fire in the rain?

McTEAGUE: People have ways.

(Pause)

TRINA: Bring me a fish. All I've eaten is oatmeal mush. For weeks.

McTEAGUE: You got *five thousand dollars*, Trina. You got three hundred right there.

TRINA: *(Snapping her fingers)* It could vanish like THAT.

McTEAGUE: SO COULD WE. *(Pause)* Go buy yourself a fish.

(McTEAGUE exits. TRINA pulls a coin out of her bag. She polishes it in her lap. Then she puts it to her lips and bites it. Then she pops it into her mouth. She sits a moment, the coin in her mouth. Then she takes the coin out, and looks at it. She puts the coin back in the bag, cinching it shut. Then she looks out.)

TRINA: You sit on a rock in the rain? Mac... Please bring me a fish...

(4)

(GRANNIS and MISS BAKER are side by side, between them the unseen wall. She holds a cup of tea, but she doesn't drink; she listens to him, who sits in his chair doing nothing. He begins, very quietly, to cry. Instinctively, she gets up and exits. A moment later she's back, with a tiny tray, on which are two cups of tea. She leaves her room, and stands outside his door.)

MISS BAKER: Mister Grannis?

(GRANNIS *doesn't hear* MISS BAKER. *She enters his room, at last, and approaches him, trembling.*)

MISS BAKER: I was making some tea, and I thought you would like a cup.

(GRANNIS *looks up at her, startled, wiping his eyes.*)

GRANNIS: What did you say?

MISS BAKER: I was making some tea, and I thought you would like a cup.

GRANNIS: I don't understand.

MISS BAKER: I was making some tea and I thought… (*She's shaking so much that the cups are rattling.*)

(GRANNIS *stares at* MISS BAKER.)

MISS BAKER: Forgive me, I only meant—but I know it must look—you probably think—I'll go—

GRANNIS: Stop!

(MISS BAKER *stops, trembling still.*)

GRANNIS: I couldn't believe it was you. I thought I was dreaming.

MISS BAKER: I wouldn't have spilled the tea. In a dream.

GRANNIS: Do you want to unencumber, of course, and I let you stand there, please, allow me… (*He takes the tray and puts it down on his chair.*)

MISS BAKER: Thank you. I thought you might like some tea. There it is. Goodbye—

GRANNIS: No, wait! …Wait.

(MISS BAKER *stops, unable to look at* GRANNIS.)

GRANNIS: I've been so lonely tonight. And last night. And last year. And the year before that. And all my life.

MISS BAKER: I've forgotten the sugar.

GRANNIS: I never take sugar.

MISS BAKER: It's cold. And I've spilled so much—

GRANNIS: I can drink from the saucer.

(Pause)

MISS BAKER: You were crying.

GRANNIS: Was I? Ah—reviewing the picnic.

MISS BAKER: Don't...

GRANNIS: You thought I was cowardly.

MISS BAKER: No. I didn't.

GRANNIS: Then why did you treat me so sharply?

MISS BAKER: I thought you were old.

(Pause)

GRANNIS: I am old.

MISS BAKER: And I realized I was, too. And I wondered how many more nights we might have. To sit on either side of the wall. And bind magazines. And drink tea. And never speak.

(Pause)

GRANNIS: How brave you were, to come to my room.

MISS BAKER: No more than you, to let me.

(Pause)

GRANNIS: Tea?

(GRANNIS hands MISS BAKER a cup; then he takes the other. Both of them pour spilled tea from the saucers into the cups.)

MISS BAKER: It *is* cold.

GRANNIS: It's nectar. Cheers.

(GRANNIS and MISS BAKER clink cups, staring into each other's eyes.)

(5)

(The McTeagues' *new room.)*

(Inside, Trina *is counting a pile of coins in her lap.)*

(In the hall outside, the Fancy Dentist *is carting off the giant tooth, when he runs into* McTeague, *who's drunk.)*

McTeague: I believe that's mine.

Fancy Dentist: It useta be. Your wife just sold it, crown and root.

McTeague: It wasn't hers to sell.

Fancy Dentist: Then she lied. She said she bought it awhile ago.

McTeague: She did—but she gave it to me.

Fancy Dentist: Well, look—I don't want to be stirring the marital waters. You want, you can buy it back.

McTeague: For how much?

Fancy Dentist: I just paid five. And I'll sell for the same.

McTeague: Where the hell would I get five dollars?

Fancy Dentist: Ask your better half. *(He tips his hat and exits with the big tooth.)*

(As McTeague *steps into his room,* Trina *hurriedly drops the coins she was counting into the chamois bag.)*

McTeague: You notice sumthin'?

Trina: You're drunk again.

McTeague: That ain't it. Look around—greasy walls, dirty sink and grimy bed, sumthin' missing…

Trina: The rent was…

McTeague: Didn't there used to be a big, golden tooth?

Trina: The rent was due.

McTEAGUE: You owe me five dollars.

TRINA: No.

McTEAGUE: That tooth was a GIFT. I want five dollars.

TRINA: NO.

(McTEAGUE *suddenly grabs* TRINA*'s hand and bites her fingers.*)

TRINA: Oh, god, don't HURT me—

(*With a jerk,* McTEAGUE *grabs the bag from her and pours a cascade of coins onto the floor.* TRINA *gasps.*)

McTEAGUE: Don't you see? I could take it all.

(TRINA, *frantic, gets down on hands and knees to scoop the coins up, sweeping them back in the bag.* McTEAGUE *grabs her by the hair, and she stops.*)

McTEAGUE: I could take it all.

TRINA: Why don't you?

(McTEAGUE *stares at* TRINA.)

TRINA: You don't love me. (*She puts her damaged hand to his face.*) Since I gave myself to you—so long ago— you've loved me less.

McTEAGUE: And you love me?

(TRINA *starts to cry.*)

McTEAGUE: Don't cry. (*Pause*) Why are you crying?

TRINA: Because I used to love you. Everything goes away.

McTEAGUE: It don't matter.

(TRINA *touches his mouth with her fingers.*)

TRINA: Open.

(McTEAGUE *opens his mouth and* TRINA *slides her fingers inside.*)

TRINA: Bite down...bite!

(MCTEAGUE *bites* TRINA*'s hand again; she moans, pulling her fingers away. He pushes her down, on top of the pile of coins, then he lets himself down on top of her. She rolls over, so he's embracing her back, and starts to laugh—a deeply unnerving laugh. He continues embracing her, kissing her neck and hair.*)

(6)

(MCTEAGUE *and* TRINA *are sprawled on the floor, asleep, having just made love.*)

(*Outside their door, in the hall,* MARIA *hovers, trying to hear. Beside her is a small satchel.*)

(ZERKOW *enters and watches. He carries the bag of junk* MARIA *hid.*)

ZERKOW: What do you hear?

(MARIA, *frightened, turns to face her husband.*)

MARIA: They move, they never pay me.

ZERKOW: Why do you need the money? Going away?

MARIA: (*Of the satchel*) This? It's junk I find. For you.

ZERKOW: At one o'clock in the morning?

MARIA: I call it a day.

(MARIA *starts to leave,* ZERKOW *grabs her, showing her his bag.*)

ZERKOW: Look!

MARIA: I don't know what that is.

ZERKOW: It's gold. More than a hundred pieces. All your gold.

MARIA: Maybe you lost your mind.

ZERKOW: Did I?

MARIA: I heard you ate a man.

ZERKOW: A man died in my arms, is all that occurred. He didn't end up on my plate.

MARIA: How did he die?

ZERKOW: We were working a stream. And it might have panned out. So we stayed too late. And the snow was too deep. And he got a fever. I held him in my arms. *(Pause)* I kept him alive for a week with stories.

MARIA: Like what?

ZERKOW: Like I told him we'd found the mother lode. And the sun on all our gold was so bright, it was melting the snow just as fast as it fell. *(Pause)* He stopped askin' for food. But he kept on askin' for stories.

MARIA: Like you.

ZERKOW: And then you stopped telling `em.

MARIA: I came to my senses.

ZERKOW: And then I died.

MARIA: Don't die…

ZERKOW: And I want you with me.

MARIA: Please. Nobody ever loved me. All my life. Except you.

ZERKOW: Then why did you let me die.

MARIA: I didn't.

ZERKOW: You didn't? *(He suddenly swings the bag of junk and brings it crashing down, right next to her.)*

(Frightened, MARIA trips and falls to the stage.)

ZERKOW: More'n a hundred pieces, and all of 'em gold. Say it.

MARIA: No.

ZERKOW: SAY IT! *(He strikes the stage with the bag again, narrowly missing her.)*

(The sound wakes McTeague, *who sits up on the floor.)*

McTeague: Who's there?

Maria: It's tin.

Zerkow: It's GOLD.

*(*Maria, *whimpering, crawls away, pursued by* Zerkow.*)*

*(*McTeague *steps out in the hall, looks around, shrugs and reenters his room. He watches his sleeping wife a moment. Then he retrieves the chamois bag and quietly starts to pick up all the coins, stuffing them in the sack. Gingerly, he slides out a few coins from under* Trina's *arms and legs. When he's done, he cinches the sack and tiptoes out.)*

*(*Trina *sleeps on.)*

(From offstage and far away, there comes a bone-chilling scream. Trina *wakes and sits up on the floor, in a panic.)*

Trina: Mac? *(Then she realizes the coins are gone. She frantically feels around the empty stage.)* Mac! The money is gone! Where is it? WHERE IS MY MONEY? MAC???

(7)

*(*Trina's *new room, above a kindergarten.)*

*(*Trina, *in a dirty robe, sits on a cot, looking out the window. She wears a fingerless glove on her right hand; two of her fingers are missing.)*

*(*Miss Baker *appears.)*

Miss Baker: Mrs McTeague?

Trina: Go away.

Miss Baker: I came when I heard.

Trina: I'm better, now. You can go. *(Pause)* Or stay and stare at my hand.

MISS BAKER: I'm sorry—I had no idea, I heard you had a brain fever, nobody mentioned blood poisoning, was it?…

TRINA: It could have been worse, the doctor said. I might have lost the whole hand.

MISS BAKER: But how can you hold your knife to carve…

TRINA: I can't. I can hold a scrubbing-brush. I take care of the kindergarten downstairs. I go entire days without hearing my voice. Nobody knows who I am.

(Pause)

MISS BAKER: And your husband has never come back?

TRINA: No. He's gone. And all the cash I'd scrimped and pinched to save…

MISS BAKER: But the lottery money is safe?…

TRINA: It's safe. It's here in this room.

(MISS BAKER *is startled.)*

MISS BAKER: I thought you'd invested it—

TRINA: What if the company vanished?

(Pause)

MISS BAKER: But it's such a lot to have on one's person—

TRINA: I needed it close. I couldn't sleep.

(Pause)

MISS BAKER: What can I do to help you?

TRINA: Let me lie. Maria was right—you hump your back and it's soonest over.

MISS BAKER: You know about Maria?

TRINA: She's dead. That's all I know.

MISS BAKER: She was beaten to death. And her husband's body was found the next morning. Washed up along the Embarcadero. Holding a sack of rusty dishes. So much for humping your back.

TRINA: Have you gloated enough? I'm tired.

MISS BAKER: I think you should take your money and go far away.

TRINA: Where?

MISS BAKER: It doesn't matter. Get on a steamer. Sail around the world.

TRINA: Oh, yes, I can see myself now...in a deckchair, wrapped in my fur, holding a cup of hot tea with three fingers...my parents moved to New Zealand last month, I can wave as my ship steams past...

MISS BAKER: New Zealand?

TRINA: His business failed. They asked me to help them out. I said no... The last letter I ever could write. I wrote, "No". *(Pause)* Nobody ever escapes.

MISS BAKER: I have.

TRINA: —Now that it doesn't matter. How long have you got?

MISS BAKER: I'm getting married.

TRINA: To what? To Death in a suit?

MISS BAKER: To Mister Grannis.

(TRINA starts laughing. MISS BAKER, embarrassed, looks around.)

MISS BAKER: It's not a bad room.

TRINA: No, it's nice. High up. With the trees outside. Sometimes I watch the children play in the courtyard...

MISS BAKER: Did you ever want to have children?

TRINA: No. Did you?

(Pause)

MISS BAKER: The sun is almost gone. I have to get back.

TRINA: It was kind of you to come…

MISS BAKER: …but you'd rather I didn't return.

(Pause)

TRINA: I go whole days without hearing my voice. It's better.

*(*MISS BAKER *nods and exits.)*

*(*TRINA *pulls a large and heavy sack from under her cot. She pours an enormous torrent of coins, onto the cot. Then she steps out of her ratty robe. Naked, she lies on the bed of money, scooping the coins up and letting them trickle over her body.)*

(Below, outside her window, McTEAGUE *appears. He looks like he's slept in a gutter for days.)*

McTEAGUE: Trina!

*(*TRINA *sits up, as coins cascade to the floor.)*

McTEAGUE: Say, Trina, it's me! Down in the courtyard. Let me in, will ya?

TRINA: *(So low he can't hear)* No. *(She starts frantically stuffing the coins back in the sack.)*

McTEAGUE: I haven't slept in a Christian bed for two weeks. And I'm starving. Trina?

TRINA: NO!

McTEAGUE: I haven't eaten since yesterday morning—

TRINA: Where's the four hundred you stole from me?

McTEAGUE: I spent it all. I've been sleeping out on the street. Will you let me in?

TRINA: No!

MCTEAGUE: Then give me some money—a little? A dollar? Give me half a dollar—a dime. For a cup of coffee.

TRINA: No.

MCTEAGUE: I wouldn't let a *dog* go hungry—

TRINA: Not even if he'd bit you?

MCTEAGUE: Come to the window. Please.

(Uncertainly, TRINA *throws her robe on and crosses to the window, to look at* MCTEAGUE.*)*

TRINA: You beat me, and bit me, and stole my money, and ended my life—except it goes on, like I was in hell—and now you just want to come back, like nothing had happened?

MCTEAGUE: *This* is what happened—I'm starving. I got nowhere to sleep. Will you give me some money or something to eat? Will you let me in?

(Pause)

TRINA: No.

*(*MCTEAGUE *stares at* TRINA.*)*

MCTEAGUE: If I had hold of you for a minute, by God, I'd make you dance. And I will. I will yet.

*(*MCTEAGUE *exits.* TRINA *stands at the window, looking out.)*

TRINA: He did look hungry… I ought to have given him something… What's happened to me? *(She calls out:)* Mac? Oh, MAC!…

(But MCTEAGUE's *gone.)*

(8)

(The kindergarten class-room. Night)

(TRINA is down on hands and knees, in her dirty robe and apron, scrubbing the floor with her damaged hands.)

(Something suddenly makes TRINA look up. MCTEAGUE is standing across the room.)

MCTEAGUE: What happened to your hair? You useta have beautiful hair.

TRINA: I don't have any money.

MCTEAGUE: You got five thousand dollars.

TRINA: I never did.

MCTEAGUE: When I was standin' outside your window—you think I'm just a dumb zinc-plugger? Do you?

TRINA: I never thought that. I love you.

(Pause)

MCTEAGUE: When I was standin' outside—

TRINA: I *love* you, Mac.

MCTEAGUE: What happened to your hand?

(TRINA doesn't respond.)

MCTEAGUE: Could you hear my insides rumblin'?

TRINA: When?

MCTEAGUE: I hadn't eat for two days. So I stood below your window. And I saw the light of your gold—

TRINA: You didn't.

MCTEAGUE: Glinting on your ceiling. Like light on running water.

TRINA: You musta been dreaming.

McTEAGUE: I know that light. I used to work in the mines. A long time back.

TRINA: A car-boy.

McTEAGUE: That's what I was. A car-boy.

(Pause)

TRINA: What *is* a car-boy, Mac? *(She starts to laugh.)*

McTEAGUE: You never knew?

(TRINA shakes her head, still laughing.)

McTEAGUE: That's all you cared.

TRINA: What are you now? *(This almost sets her off again, but she holds it in.)* What did you useta be? A car-boy in a mine. What'll you be five minutes from now? I don't know. I never knew. *(Pause)* What'll I be five minutes from now?

McTEAGUE: A dead woman. *(Pause)* You useta be so proud of your hair. It's a rat's nest.

(Pause)

TRINA: That paint I used on the animals, Mac? "Nonpoisonous" paint? It wasn't.

McTEAGUE: You drink it?

TRINA: It got in my blood. My fingers were always raw...

McTEAGUE: Say why.

TRINA: It don't matter.

McTEAGUE: It matters to *me*!

TRINA: You'd bite 'em.

McTEAGUE: Why?

TRINA: I never knew.

(McTEAGUE hits TRINA, out of the blue. She's so startled she barely reacts.)

McTEAGUE: Because you got five thousand dollars, Trina. Shining out your window at night like a lighthouse light. And all that money means to you is get down on your bitten-off hands and your watery knees, day before Christmas Eve, all alone, and scrub a floor a thousand leaking brats have mucked so many times it won't ever come clean—for what? All alone on your knees in gray water. For what? A dollar more. Five thousand. Five thousand and *one*. Which you might's well give me right now.

TRINA: They don't pay me a dollar a day, are you out of your— *(She stops herself.)*

McTEAGUE: I saw this battle-ax give you a dollar. This lady all prinked out—

TRINA: What lady?

McTEAGUE: Black bombazine. Glass grapes on her hat. Looked like a funeral barge gone aground. From the Kindergarten Board, I figured. Gave you a Christmas bonus, right?

(TRINA shakes her head.)

McTEAGUE: Don't shake your bean. I saw you through the classroom window. Bowin' and scrapin'. Kissin' her creamy hand.

TRINA: I didn't kiss her hand.

(McTEAGUE hits TRINA again. She backs away.)

McTEAGUE: Her hand with all the fingers on it. Diamond rings. "*Thank* you for letting me scrub the floor where little Johnny threw up last week. A dollar? Don't give me a *dollar*. I'd do this just for the joy of the mortifaction!" *(Pause)* Give me the dollar, then.

TRINA: Nobody gave me a dollar—

McTEAGUE: GIVE IT TO ME.

(McTeague *grabs at* Trina's *apron, ripping a pocket. A silver dollar falls to the floor. They stare at it.*)

McTeague: Pick it up.

(Hesitantly, Trina *picks it up.)*

McTeague: Now what do you want to do with it?

Trina: Give it to you. *(She offers him the coin.)*

McTeague: You can't.

Trina: Why not?

McTeague: Because nobody gave you a dollar.

(Trina *offers it again.)*

Trina: Here!

(McTeague *knocks it out of* Trina's *hand, with a roar.)*

McTeague: NOBODY GAVE YOU A DOLLAR. *(Pause)* Nobody gave you anything. *(Pause)* So here you are. Aren't you? HERE YOU ARE.

(Pause)

Trina: You stole my money.

McTeague: Eighty bucks.

Trina: Walked out on me. All that money I scrimped and pinched to save—

McTeague: Just eighty bucks. After all those years. That's all you said you could hold together—

Trina: It mighta been more…

McTeague: You told me eighty bucks.

(Pause)

Trina: I'm not askin' for anything back—

McTeague: Good. It was only the eighty. Didn't last that long. I had me a lobster or two. I saw a few shows. I rode the ferry. All gone.

TRINA: Then it's gone. I don't ask for it back—

McTEAGUE: That's *good*. Now give me the rest.

TRINA: The rest is still invested, Mac—

McTEAGUE: At your fat old uncle's?

(TRINA *nods.*)

McTEAGUE: I talked to your fat old uncle. *(Pause)* He thought we'd had a lover's spat. He thought I was trying to win you back. He told me where I could find you. He told me where I could find your money, too.

(Pause)

TRINA: *(A question)* You don't want to win me back.

McTEAGUE: Well—I stood outside your window. I'd been sleeping dead on the street for a week. Got beaten up twice. I was so hungry, the night you saw me, my knees kept giving way. You would have thrown a dog that *down* a piece of gristle. What did you throw *me*, Trina?

TRINA: You left me. And I was sick. I could have died.

(Pause)

McTEAGUE: I want the money. All of it. Now. The last nickel.

TRINA: It isn't here.

McTEAGUE: It's not at your uncle's. He told me so. Is it anywhere?

(As if turning her back on a rattling snake, TRINA begins to scrub the floor again.)

McTEAGUE: Nobody gave you five thousand dollars.

TRINA: That's right.

McTEAGUE: Nobody gave you anything.

TRINA: So here I am. *(Pause)* I'd dream about you. After you left.

McTeague: What was I doing?

Trina: Dancing, in a shower of gold.

McTeague: *Your* gold.

Trina: I guess. *(As if hoping he were getting ready to go:)* Goodnight, Mac.

(McTeague watches Trina scrub as she tries to ignore him.)

Trina: Goodnight.

(McTeague crosses to Trina and stands above her.)

McTeague: For the last time...

(Trina keeps scrubbing.)

McTeague: Will you give me the money?

(Trina stops scrubbing, looks out. She shakes her head; McTeague stares at her. She looks down at the floor and starts scrubbing again.)

(The lights fade to black.)

(9)

(In the Panamint Mountains. Night)

(Cribbens, a grumpy but decent-hearted prospector, is panning for gold. As he sloshes water in his pan, he sings.)

Cribbens:
"Did you ever hear tell of sweet Betsy from Pike..."
(He looks in his pan, disheartened.) Lotta sand. Fool's gold. About what I deserve. *(He dips his pan in the stream again and sings.)*
"...who crossed the wide prairies with her lover Ike..."
(He looks again in his pan, disgusted with himself.)
Coulda been any number a things. Oh, no. Had to be a pros-pec-tor, leave my family, end up mad as a June bug, talkin' trash to myself an' the empty— *(He*

stops talking suddenly, cocking an ear.) Who's there? *(There's no answer. He pulls out a revolver.)* Goddammit, somebody's there. I can tell, I been up in these hills long enough, come OUT!

(MCTEAGUE *steps out of the shadows—a pack on his back and the bird cage in one hand.)*

MCTEAGUE: Don't shoot. I ain't a claim-jumper.

CRIBBENS: The hell you say.

MCTEAGUE: Just passing through.

CRIBBENS: I been up in these hills too long, I guess. *(Pointing at* MCTEAGUE*)* I keep thinkin' I see a man standin' there. With a bird cage.

(MCTEAGUE *shrugs.)*

CRIBBENS: Just out for a stroll?

MCTEAGUE: I grew up in a mining camp, other side of that ridge. It's been a long time since I had me a look.

CRIBBENS: The Golden Spike?

(MCTEAGUE *nods.)*

CRIBBENS: That mine played out a few years ago. And the camp blew away.

MCTEAGUE: Oh. Well…I just wanted to… Hear that sound? Like somethin roarin', way far off…

CRIBBENS: Like surf? You know what it is?

MCTEAGUE: It's the mountains.

CRIBBENS: Yep.

MCTEAGUE: It's the sound they make in the night. I remember.

*(*CRIBBENS, *deciding to trust* MCTEAGUE, *puts his gun away.)*

CRIBBENS: That why you came back?

McTEAGUE: I don't know. I *don't* know. Just passing through. *(He starts to exit.)*

CRIBBENS: You useta be a horse doctor. True?

(McTEAGUE turns to face the prospector, puzzled.)

CRIBBENS: And this stablekeeper turned you in, so you couldn't practice no more. Don't ask me why. So you done for him with a pitchfork. And now yer workin' yer way to Arizona.

(McTEAGUE is almost amused by this legend.)

McTEAGUE: That the story bout me in town?

CRIBBENS: Course I said, "Don't be a horses patoot. How hard'd it be to nail a man on the lam with a bird cage?"

(McTEAGUE stares at CRIBBENS. He puts down the bird cage.)

McTEAGUE: When the law comes by—will you tell `em you saw me?

CRIBBENS: Saw who?

(Pause. McTEAGUE considers a moment, then picks the bird cage back up.)

McTEAGUE: *(Explaining his action)* If they find me, well—they find me.

(CRIBBENS points out.)

CRIBBENS: Not if you go that way. *Nobody'll* find you. `Cepting the random vulture.

McTEAGUE: Why?

CRIBBENS: That way's Death Valley. Which ain't a poetical name. Its descriptive.

McTEAGUE: Didn't somebody strike out there?

CRIBBENS: Yessir. To the tune of a million or so. Gold Hill. Clear across. But you wouldn't go east to cross it,

though. You'd have to head south, to the Amergosa.
And wait for the winter runoff. And follow that out.
Be in Gold Hill next year or so. That's the only way to
work it. Other, you'd fry.

McTEAGUE: *(Thinking this through)* But so would
anyone else, if they tried to come after me… *(Pause)*
What'd you do with a million dollars?

CRIBBENS: Get laid. *(Pause)* I had a wife and a child one
time. I'd find `em. *(Pause)* You?

(McTEAGUE doesn't answer.)

CRIBBENS: Must be *somethin'* you dream about.

McTEAGUE: I don't dream. *(He now heads off, bird cage in
hand, for a final time.)*

*(CRIBBENS watches him go exactly where he warned him not
to.)*

CRIBBENS: You son-of-a… Hey! Hey, you!

*(McTEAGUE, long gone, doesn't answer. CRIBBENS watches
him disappear, appalled.)*

CRIBBENS: DON'T GO EAST, YOU SON-OF-A-BITCH!
DON'T GO—…

*(Defeated, CRIBBENS watches McTEAGUE descending into
Death Valley.)*

(10)

(Death Valley. Noon. Blinding light)

*(McTEAGUE comes on—his shirt stripped off and soaked
with sweat. He stops and shields his eyes to look up at the
sun.)*

McTEAGUE: I never knew it could get as hot as this.
(Pause) I don't think this is gonna work out so well.
(He puts the cage and his bedroll down.) If it gets much

hotter… (*He shakes his canteen to hear how much is left. He starts to take a drink, then stops. Instead, he sprinkles some water onto the sacks that cover the bird cage.*) Maybe get under a blanket, just take a nap… (*He takes his blanket out and drapes one end across the bird cage. Then he starts to crawl under. He makes the mistake of touching the ground with his hand. He jerks his hand away, screaming in pain.*) I *knew*. I could feel it coming up through my shoes, I ain't thinking… (*He stares at the bird cage, suddenly snatches it up.*) I ain't *thinking*! Don't put you down, you'll fry like an egg. Lord! What a country. (*He folds the blanket and puts it on the hot ground and then sets the bird cage on top of it.*)

(*As he does this,* TRINA *enters, her back to* MCTEAGUE)

(MCTEAGUE *senses her presence, but doesn't turn to face her.*)

MCTEAGUE: Not even a rock to hide under…so there *can't* be nobody followin' me, if there was, I'd see em a day away. (*He looks in every direction except where* TRINA *is.*) And who'd follow me anyway? Who'd be fool enough to try?… (*More and more nervous, he strains to catch some sound.*) But I *hear* something… Don't I? (*He stares out.*) Who's there? Will you show yourselves? *Will* you? Let's have it out, now. Come on. (*He draws his gun.*) I won't be afraid if you'll only come on. Come ON! (*Finally he fires—at nothing—and fires again and again, till the gun is empty.*)

(*Now* TRINA *turns to face* MCTEAGUE, *who still doesn't look at her. She's bloody and bruised.*)

TRINA: What are you shooting at?

(MCTEAGUE, *who's always sensed* TRINA *was there, is not surprised to hear her talk.*)

MCTEAGUE: Nobody's there. I don't know. They ain't comin'. How could they? Bottom of a dead ocean.

That's what this was. (*Pause. He turns to face her, finally and he has no reaction to seeing how battered she is.*)

TRINA: (*Looking around*) Don't you love the ocean?

McTEAGUE: That ain't the water, it's light on the sand…

TRINA: I'd like to go off in one of those great big sailing ships. Just away and away and away…

McTEAGUE: Where?

TRINA: Anywhere. If I had enough money—

(McTEAGUE *suddenly screams. Unnerved by the violence of his own cry, he turns away.*)

(TRINA *starts to disappear.*)

(*Desperate,* McTEAGUE *remembers a moment long ago.*)

McTEAGUE: A strand of your hair, got caught on my ring…

TRINA: It didn't hurt.

McTEAGUE: Well, that's fine…

(*Afraid his memories will make him weaker,* McTEAGUE *now tries to act as if* TRINA *had never been there, talking again to his bird.*)

McTEAGUE: If it gets much hotter…

(TRINA *is gone.* McTEAGUE *is alone again in the desert.*)

McTEAGUE: I ain't got any too much of my water left. (*Pause*) If it gets much hotter, I don't know what I'll do. (*Pause*) I gotta get out of this place in a hurry, sure. (*Now he finally looks at where* TRINA *was, and sees she's gone. Trina? (No answer. He stares out.)* Listen: no twigs rustling, nothing moving, insects, wind. Not a sound… (*His mind drifts, thinking again of* TRINA:) Last week I could hear you holding your breath for an *hour*…a strand of your hair…

(Unconsciously seeking comfort, McTEAGUE *uncaps his canteen.)*

(At that moment MARCUS *enters—dressed in a fancy cowboy getup, covered with dust and sweat. He aims a gun at* McTEAGUE.)

MARCUS: I got one bullet left. It's yours.

*(*McTEAGUE *glances at* MARCUS, *not curious, and then takes a sip of water.)*

MARCUS: Put the canteen down. You son of a bitch.

*(*McTEAGUE *recaps the canteen and then starts to exit, ignoring* MARCUS.)

MARCUS: McTEAGUE!

*(*McTEAGUE *is almost off.* MARCUS *shoots.* McTEAGUE's *canteen goes flying off.* McTEAGUE *turns and stares at* MARCUS.)

McTEAGUE: *(Puzzled)* Marcus?

MARCUS: Who the hell did you think I was?

*(*McTEAGUE *doesn't answer.)*

MARCUS: Where's the money?

*(*McTEAGUE *throws down a saddlebag.* MARCUS *grabs it and gives it a shake, to hear the jingle.)*

MARCUS: Got it at last!

McTEAGUE: You got any water?

MARCUS: No.

McTEAGUE: We're dead men, then.

(Pause)

MARCUS: My horse gave out a half-mile back. We could drink his blood. It's been done before.

McTEAGUE: I ain't that thirsty yet. *(Pause)* So you ended up a cowboy.

MARCUS: Didn't I say I would?

MCTEAGUE: Are you lost?

MARCUS: Last Saturday night I went to town. And I saw a description of you. On a poster.

MCTEAGUE: Easy as that?

MARCUS: How hard do you reckon it ought to be, to track a man with a bird cage under his arm?

MCTEAGUE: You came alone?

MARCUS: I was with a posse. Deputized. They followed you to the edge of the desert. And then they saw your footprints heading out into the alkali. They gave you up for gone.

MCTEAGUE: I was. I am. *(Pause)* Let's be moving along, somewhere.

MARCUS: Where? We're a hundred miles from anywhere. What's the good of moving on?

MCTEAGUE: What's the good of stopping here?

(Pause)

MARCUS: We're done for. Ain't we?

MCTEAGUE: Why'd you follow me into this place?

MARCUS: I wanted what was mine.

(Pause)

MCTEAGUE: I ain't so sure about who that money belongs to.

MARCUS: The one with the gun.

MCTEAGUE: You said you had one shot left. You fired.

(Pause. MARCUS shifts his gun, holding it now like a club, as MCTEAGUE approaches.)

MARCUS: You soldiered me out of that money once. It's my turn, now.

(McTEAGUE *suddenly shoves at* MARCUS, *who stumbles over the birdcage and falls to the ground. In a second,* McTEAGUE *is on top of his enemy, wrestling for the gun.*)

(McTEAGUE *gets it at last and clubs* MARCUS. *For a moment,* MARCUS *lies still;* McTEAGUE *lays next to him, panting. With a final quiver of energy,* MARCUS *grabs his opponent's wrist. We hear a click.* McTEAGUE *doesn't seem to realize what's happened. As he gets to his feet, he feels a tug at his wrist. He looks down.* MARCUS *has handcuffed himself to* McTEAGUE. McTEAGUE *stares out.*)

McTEAGUE: One hundred miles… (*He looks down at* MARCUS.) Which way is your horse…Marcus?

(McTEAGUE *pulls at* MARCUS; MARCUS *is dead.*)

(*The bird in the cage begins to feebly sing.*)

McTEAGUE: What's the good of stopping here? (*He looks off.*) How far…

(*As* McTEAGUE *stands there, cuffed to a dead man, listening to the bird, the light starts to fade.*)

McTEAGUE: Listen…insects, wind…nothing.

(*The bird sings on.*)

McTEAGUE: Don't stop. (*Pause*) It'll get cooler. Dark… (*Pause*) Don't stop…

(*The lights fade to black.*)

END OF PLAY

www.ingramcontent.com/pod-product-compliance
Lightning Source LLC
Chambersburg PA
CBHW052108090426
42741CB00009B/1723